Y0-CAS-402

WHY WE THINK
AS WE DO

WHY WE THINK AS WE DO

ROBERT A. LISTON

Franklin Watts

New York | London | 1977

Library of Congress Cataloging in
Publication Data

Liston, Robert A.
  Why we think as we do.

  Bibliography: p.
  Includes index.
  SUMMARY: Examines how propaganda
attempts to influence opinions, the way
public information offices and the mass
media can promote propaganda, and the
reaction of the American public.
  1. Propaganda—Juvenile literature.
2. Public opinion—Juvenile literature.
3. Advertising—Juvenile literature.
[1. Propaganda. 2. Public opinion.
3. Advertising.] I. Title.
HM263.L54   301.15'4   77-23271
ISBN 0-531-00390-6

To Dick and Marie Strait

ACKNOWLEDGMENTS

I would like to thank the staffs of the Trumbull and Westport, Connecticut, public libraries for the many books they made available to me—and their patience in awaiting their return. Most special thanks go to my good friend Richard L. Gilman of the University of Bridgeport Library who also provided many excellent books. Another friend, David O. Strickland, provided much helpful information and advice. Betty Anne Peterzell, of Stamford, Connecticut, and Eleanor R. Seagraves, of Washington, D. C., were also of assistance. My wife, Jean, and daughter, Felicia, helped with the manuscript.

CONTENTS

CHAPTER ONE   A Matter of Opinion

During his 1972 campaign for president, Senator George S. McGovern of South Dakota appeared at a football game. This has become standard campaign practice, along with kissing babies, wearing Indian headdresses, and waving at crowds in parades. When Senator McGovern was introduced to the crowd at this particular football game, a wave of boos swept the stands, eventually falling on his ears as thunder.

Why was he booed? Senator McGovern was (and is) known to be an honorable man, a family man, with a reputation for integrity. As the Democratic nominee, he had arrived at the second highest honor the nation can bestow, the only higher being given to the person elected president. He had won the nomination of the majority party by legitimate means. And yet he was booed. He took the booing personally. It was to him an expression not of disagreement with his politics, but of personal dislike for him and what he was as a person. He was deeply hurt.

In asking why that crowd booed, we are really asking why we Americans think as we do. We honor our democracy and our free elections. We generally tend to respect people of stature, even when we disagree with them. What led that crowd to boo a nominee for president?

Those boos were hardly an isolated instance of the fickleness of collective American thinking. Our last two *elected* presidents *

---

* President Gerald R. Ford is the only man in history not elected either president or vice-president. Mr. Ford, long-time Republican leader in the House of Representatives, was nominated vice-president by Mr. Nixon following the resignation on October 12, 1973, of the elected vice-president,

—Lyndon B. Johnson in 1964 and Richard M. Nixon in 1972—
were swept into office by the largest popular majorities in history.
More than 60 percent of those voting chose them over their opponents. Yet, each man became highly unpopular and was in effect
driven from office. Mr. Johnson became unpopular because of the
war in Vietnam and chose not to seek another term. Mr. Nixon
resigned rather than face certain impeachment for his role in the
massive scandal known as Watergate. Why did our attitudes
toward these two presidents change so abruptly and sharply? Why
do we think as we do?

In August 1964, Congress passed the Gulf of Tonkin Resolution
approving and supporting the "determination of the President . . .
to take all necessary measures to repel any armed attack against
the forces of the United States and to prevent further aggression." The resolution passed the House unanimously and the Senate
with only two dissenting votes following an alleged attack on
American destroyers in the Gulf of Tonkin off Vietnam. Within a
few years, many who had voted for the resolution had become
vocal opponents of the war it authorized. Several important steps
were taken in Congress to end the war and to curtail the power of
presidents to take the nation into war. Why was the war in Vietnam supported so strongly, and why did attitudes change?

Today black Americans hold posts on the Supreme Court, are
members of the Senate and House, and serve in many other positions of influence. Several top-rated shows on television are about
black families. Black actors, artists, writers, composers, and per-

Spiro T. Agnew. Mr. Agnew resigned after pleading "no contest" to charges
of income-tax fraud. Mr. Ford was sworn in on December 6, 1973, after
being confirmed by both the House and Senate. His appointment as vice-
president was the first under the Twenty-Fifth Amendment to the Constitution. Mr. Ford then became president on August 9, 1974, after Mr.
Nixon resigned. Nelson A. Rockefeller, former governor of New York,
was then nominated vice-president by Mr. Ford and confirmed by Congress.

formers are widely admired. Black history is now taught routinely in schools. While far from eliminated, racial tensions in the United States have considerably abated from the late 1960s when the nation was plagued with racial murders, riots, burnings, bombings, and other forms of violence. What caused the change?

A quarter century ago, DDT was hailed as a miracle insecticide that would free the earth from insect pests. Today its use is virtually banned in the United States, along with several other pesticides. In the late 1940s and 1950s, Americans began a "flight to the suburbs," turning lush farmland into housing tracts. By 1975, so many Americans were leaving urban and suburban areas for farms and rural areas that experts called it the greatest decline in urban populations since the founding of the nation. Why these changing attitudes?

One more example. Throughout history, the United States disarmed after each of its wars. Americans distrusted a standing military force. Beginning in 1950, Americans embraced the principle of national defense, dedicating the nation to maintenance of a military force of doomsday proportions. In the mid-1970s, the cost of this military machine exceeded $100 billion a year. By 1980, the annual bill is expected to exceed $150 billion. Members of Congress voted the money, convinced the public wanted it spent. Why this abrupt, even profound, change in the way Americans had always thought?

Are these changes in attitudes a spontaneous expression of public sentiment? Did inevitable events, altered situations, and fresh information cause the American people to change their thinking? Or were these changes in some way manipulated by propaganda, advertising, public relations techniques, and various forms of education or deception (depending upon the point of view) by governmental and societal leaders?

These are extremely important questions in a democracy dedicated to free expression and "government of the people, by the people, for the people," as Lincoln put it in the Gettysburg Address. All strike to the heart of what we Americans are as a people and how we govern ourselves.

It can be said at the outset that the answers to all the above questions are probably yes. Some American attitudes are spontaneous, a product of what we are as human beings and as a nationality. Other attitudes are a reaction to events, situations, and information. The real problem is not that such influences exist, but alerting Americans to the influences and to the advantages and perils of each so that we may more effectively govern ourselves. If, for example, oil companies advertise that they need high profits to develop the nation's petroleum resources, is that accurate information, an expression of the desire of Americans to have plentiful energy, or self-serving manipulation of public attitudes through advertising? It is a matter of considerable importance to Americans, if not to decide which, at least to realize that all three may be factors.

In considering such matters we are investigating public opinion. The creation and measurement of public opinion is a multi-billion dollar industry in the United States. It embraces book, magazine, and newspaper publishing, radio and television broadcasting, public relations activities, advertising in all its forms, and the mammoth public information activities of federal, state, and local governments. That is not all. Polling of public opinion is an important industry. Politicians, whether professional or amateur, deal directly with public opinion. Education, including teachers and professors, is often a leading molder of public opinion. Without a doubt, more effort and energy go into the fostering and evaluation of public opinion in the United States than in any other country, perhaps the rest of the world combined.

Yet, the object of all this activity—public opinion—remains indescribably elusive. Scholars have been hard pressed to define it, identify it, and certainly to explain it. The problem begins with the uniqueness of every human being. Just as each person's fingerprints, lip prints, and brain waves are unique, so is that person's background, experiences, and sense of himself and the world around him—or her.

Each person is a collection of opinions, some contradictory, and all subject to instantaneous change. Consider yourself. Chances are you have an opinion (more than one?) on the nation's energy crisis. You may feel we have a need to conserve energy, develop new supplies of existing fuels, such as coal and oil, and research new sources of energy, such as solar and thermal heat. You may also be very concerned about unemployment, perhaps because you face the prospect of job hunting. You may likewise have strong feeling about the environment, perhaps believing that the air, water, and earth need to be conserved and unpolluted. You may or may not be aware that in the minds of many people these opinions clash. It is argued that conserving energy and creating full employment may be opposites, impossible to reconcile. Protecting the environment and developing new energy sources may be incompatible. And all of your opinions are subject to change by events, circumstances, and information. Even while wanting a clean environment, you may decide that a new, polluting industry in town is wise because it offers you a job and lowers your property taxes.

All of us have contradictory and highly changeable opinions on many matters. To name a few: politics, foreign affairs, national defense, the economy, taxation, movies, fashions, arts, automobiles, styles of homes, and the best places to live, as well as travel, relations between parents and children, the best forms of education, books, television, movie stars, sports celebrities, and which brand of breakfast cereal tastes best.

All of us are a bundle of opinions. They roll off our lips effortlessly. Most are trivial. We like a certain television show; we dislike a particular beverage; we "Monday morning quarterback" a football game; the idea of wearing a pink suit (or whatever) is appalling or appealing to us as the case may be. We also have

opinions on matters of national and international importance—
communism, national defense, taxation, and whatever else is in the
headlines or news broadcasts. All of us sometimes utter trivial
opinions even on matters of great importance. We also tend to give
an opinion that seems appropriate to our listeners. On educational
matters, for example, the opinion we might express to students may
well be different from that expressed to teachers, the principal,
parents, or an irate taxpayer. When discussing a strike, the views
we express to a workingman might be somewhat different from
those expressed to a businessman.

Still, in all this welter of opinions, much of which qualifies as
idle chatter, there are certain things we feel strongly about. We
express our opinion vigorously. We argue our point of view, brave
disagreement with others, and even try to convince them to accept
our opinions. These are the opinions that really count.

In analyzing such opinions, scholars have attributed some characteristics to them. The opinion tends to have *direction*. We are for
or against something. We are for civil rights, against unemployment, in favor of the women's liberation movement, opposed to
gasoline rationing. The opinion also has *intensity*. We may feel
very strongly about it or be somewhat less committed to the point
of view. And the opinion may have *stability*. We have had the
opinion for a long time and we are likely to hold the opinion for
some time into the future.

When an opinion has direction, intensity, and stability, it is likely
to have a high *informational content*.* We know something about
the subject. We studied it or talked to people. Experiences affect
our thinking. For example, a person who belongs to a labor union
and has attended meetings, read union literature, and worked in a
factory is likely to have views that are different from and more
strongly held than those of a person without these experiences.

---

* These italicized terms are used by Robert E. Lane and David O. Sears
in their book, *Public Opinion*.

Also, a person whose opinion lacks information may change it when he learns some facts contrary to his beliefs.

An opinion can also be emotional in nature, as against intellectual. An intellectual opinion can be a subject for discussion, but an emotional opinion may bring a commitment. We take action. We try to convince our friends and even strangers. We join an organization, write to public officials, join a strike, boycott, or engage in some form of protest demonstration. We become *involved*.

An opinion that has direction, intensity, stability, and brings forth an emotional commitment to action is a powerful opinion indeed. Propagandists, advertisers, public relations men, and other manipulators try very hard to foster opinions of this type. Advertisers, for example, spend billions of dollars a year to convince people that they will win love and self-esteem through a superwhite wash, that a certain car will attract a girl friend or boyfriend, and that purchases of dolls, toys, and other goodies will win the love of children.

Another aim of opinion manipulators is to make many people have intense feelings about a subject. After all, it is possible for a person to have a very strong opinion about something and be the only person in the world to feel that way. There are small groups of people in the United States who are avid collectors of obscure items, or choose to live in an isolated place without electricity and other creature comforts, or worship the memory of Adolf Hitler. There are many other possible examples. In the parlance of scholars of public opinion, such views have *extremity*. This word describes unusual or nontypical opinion.

The views dominant in a society are called *modal opinion*. The majority of people hold this view. All other opinions are measured against it. The aim of opinion manipulators is to make this modal opinion be as intense, stable, and emotional as possible.

The pollsters, such as George Gallup and Louis Harris, are in the business of trying to measure modal opinions. They seek to measure by questioning a small but allegedly scientific sample of

Americans, asking how they feel about a wide range of subjects at any given moment. Gallup, for example, has conducted an ongoing poll for many years on how good a job people think the president is doing. This "popularity" poll, taken every two weeks, shows public regard for presidential performance going up and down, apparently in relation to presidential actions and the public's perception of them. Shortly after his election in 1972, President Nixon won a high rating of more than 75 percent. At the time of his resignation in August 1974, less than 30 percent approved of his performance in office. A television speech, a meeting with a Soviet or Chinese leader, favorable economic news can increase a president's popularity overnight.

Perhaps the leading example of the ephemeral nature of modal opinion involves Harry S. Truman. He was elected to office in 1948 in what many consider the greatest political upset in recent history. Yet, by January 1953, when he left office, his popularity on the Gallup Poll had shrunk to the lowest in history, 23 percent. Shortly after he returned to his home in Independence, Missouri, public regard for the ex-president began to increase. By 1975, a sort of Truman cult had developed. Several best-selling books and a play, all based on his life and words, were produced. One of the least popular presidents was being cited as an example of presidential integrity, a symbol of the "good ol' days."

Any person or organization who seeks to manipulate public opinion in America undertakes a most difficult task. Public opinion (in the sense of dominant or modal opinion) is fickle. It can change, seemingly overnight. We react to fads. We are prone to enthusiasms. A single event can lead to an instant change, even a reversal of public opinion.

Yet, we remain highly independent, reserving to ourselves our opinions on almost everything. Unanimity is almost impossible. Even the Japanese attack on Pearl Harbor, Hawaii, on December 7, 1941, did not result in a unanimous declaration of war by Congress. There was one vote against it. We tolerate, sometimes even applaud, a broad spectrum of extremist views, often granting celebrity status to iconoclasts and "odd balls."

Americans often refuse to have their opinions manipulated by those who conceive of the people as a herd to be led. Examples are legion. Thousands of new products are introduced each year and most, including many that are heavily advertised, fail to win public acceptance. Opposition to the war in Vietnam grew despite appeals by Presidents Johnson and Nixon to the patriotism of Americans and despite incessant claims that we were winning the war. In his increasingly desperate efforts to extricate himself from the Watergate scandal, Mr. Nixon made several nationwide television speeches contending that he had told all and urging the people to forget the scandal. He simply was not believed by the majority of people.

Yet, many examples suggest that Americans have a tendency to let their opinions be manipulated. We will be considering these matters in more detail later, but we can cite our sixty-year fear of communism and the wars, deaths, and vast expenditures for armaments that it has provoked; our long, self-defeating antagonism toward Blacks and Indians; our streak of violence; our long tendency to plunder the resources of our land; the notion that money and possessions mean the "good life" and the personal unhappiness as well as waste and pollution that has resulted; our fascination with technology despite growing evidence that at least some of it is harmful and self-defeating.

For good and ill, Americans have a record of being both resistant and susceptible to manipulation of their opinions. In answering the question why we think as we do, we will be examining some of the techniques—often extremely subtle—that manipulators use. We hope that by becoming aware of these techniques, we can become, if not more resistant to them, at least able to form more rational and intelligent opinions.

At the core of why we think as we do is what we are as a people. Anyone seeking to manipulate public opinion must understand how the land, the climate, our history and heritage, have shaped Americans. We come from many lands, many races, and religions. With pride, we call the United States the "melting pot" of nations. The American mind or character that resulted from all this diversity is not very easy to describe, but we can try in the next chapter.

One of the evil geniuses of history was Dr. Joseph Paul Goebbels —a name perhaps not as remembered in infamy as it ought to be. He was propaganda minister for Adolf Hitler's Nazi Germany before and during World War II. Goebbels developed or exploited the "big lie" and other propaganda techniques that led the Germans and the world into the disastrous war. In their book, *The Idea Invaders*, George N. Gordon, Irving Falk, and William Hodapp gave grudging praise to Goebbels's "managing the minds of his fellow Germans":

> . . . he managed to convince a civilized, well-educated nation with a long and impressive history of humanitarian and scientific traditions to accept a philosophy of barbarism and mysticism which, despite its attempts to exploit various facets of German history, nevertheless stood for everything antithetical to the best that could be found in German heritage.

The propaganda techniques used by Goebbels have been widely studied—and used by those who would manipulate the minds of men for the purposes of a nation or a tyrant.

Goebbels's techniques can be reduced to a few simple principles, which he adored expounding in lectures to his colleagues. First, propaganda had to be simple. He sought to find the most primitive arguments and then express them in the most popular form. For example, complex social and economic problems of pre-World War II Germany were summarily blamed on Jews, Communists, or some other enemy. When Hitler sought to invade

Czechoslovakia or seize other territory, Goebbels dreamed up some "threat" that nation posed against Germany.

Second, propaganda appealed solely to the emotions, instinct, the passions of the people. Such themes as patriotism, love of family, fear, pride in victory were exploited. Conversely, an intellectual argument was seldom used. No attempt was made, for example, to convince German intellectuals of the righteousness of Hitler's cause by rational argument.

Third, successful propaganda was incessant repetition of simple, emotional themes, slogans, and captions. The words could vary, but the message was always the same. The radio, newspapers, and billboards were constantly filled with it. He sought to use all means of communication in a "concerted effort" to propagandize. He declared that the propagandist could never "lose his voice."

Fourth, propaganda was supported by facts, but the facts were cleverly chosen with the propaganda object in mind. For example, to bolster the morale of Germans during the war, he reported Nazi victories, while omitting references to losses. Goebbels considered it important, when using fact to bolster propaganda, to present the half-truths in an objective a manner as possible. They were made believable because they were presented on regular newscasts in what appeared to be straight, unbiased reporting.

Fifth, propaganda should shield the public from unpleasant or uncomfortable facts. Omission of information was just as important, if not more so than what was reported. Thus, for a long time the German people were kept from knowing of troop losses, bombing raids, food shortages, dissatisfactions with Hitler and the Nazis. One of Goebbels's most successful omissions was concealment of Hitler's so-called "final solution" to the "Jewish problem." For a long time, most Germans did not know that Jews were being rounded up, shipped to concentration camps, and murdered. Even the existence of the camps was a well-guarded secret.

Sixth, the propagandist must lie *credibly*. Goebbels said propaganda had "nothing at all to do with truth." The sole aim of a propaganda campaign was success, and to achieve that success all was fair "in propaganda as in love." Goebbels was a master liar. But it was not just that he lied so much, but that he made the lies believable. For example, he concocted the outrageous lie that the British government had decided that if they won the war they would separate all German children from their parents and then sterilize all German males so as to wipe out the German population. Goebbels managed to have this "information" leaked in Britain so that it was actually printed as fact in the British papers. Goebbels then trumpeted these British news stories through his propaganda machine to frighten the German people into hating the British more and to fighting harder to win the war.*

The evil genius of Goebbels was in designing such simple methods of propaganda and in being so ruthless in using them. He made propaganda a kind of salesmanship applied to politics and used it to both excuse and conceal the barbarities of Nazism.

An illustration of these techniques and one of the high points of Goebbels's propaganda efforts came in 1943. Rumors of the Nazi

---

* One of the greatest and surely most influential lies of World War II was the tale that Hitler and other Nazi leaders had built an impregnable fortress in the mountains of Bavaria, where they planned a last stand against the onrushing Allied armies. General Dwight D. Eisenhower and other American commanders believed this story. Rather than racing to Berlin, American troops turned southward to attack the fortress in Bavaria. No such fortress existed. The repercussions of this lie are endless. The Russians went on to occupy Berlin and what has become East Germany. The map of Europe with a divided Germany came to exist. Many of the postwar tensions over Berlin and a divided Germany might have been avoided had American troops continued eastward. When the Russians occupied Berlin, they found the bodies of Hitler and Goebbels in a bunker. Both had committed suicide. No one knows if Goebbels concocted the lie about the nonexistent fortress that so changed postwar history. But it was precisely the sort of elaborate, credible lie that was so typical of him. In his exaggerated vanity, he would have adored having contrived a lie that would so change the world after his death.

military disaster at Stalingrad in the Soviet Union had reached Germany. Morale was at a low ebb. With Hitler's blessing, Goebbels invented a plan for "total war" and sprang it on the people in a speech at a mass rally in Berlin. The rally and the speech were pure Goebbels—a huge crowd of enthusiastic Nazi supporters, flags, slogans, martial music. To insure a properly enthusiastic response to his speech, Goebbels had the audience larded with claques to applaud and cheer upon command. He even had applause and cheers played through the loudspeaker system to make the response greater.

Goebbels's speech was a web of lies and half-truths, but masterfully concocted and presented. He began by playing on the crowd's fears of Bolshevism, as the Russian brand of communism was called in those days. He declared that Bolshevism was synonymous with "world revolution of the Jews," the "Bolshevik-capitalist tyranny," and with "terror," "anarchy," "hunger," "misery," and "slave labor." This was all lies, but cleverly done so it was exceedingly simple to understand and laden with emotional fears. A rational person might ask, "What world revolution of Jews?" How could Bolshevism and capitalism, two opposite economic ideas, be linked to form a tyranny? And wasn't Nazi Germany capitalist? Were not terror, anarchy, hunger, misery, and slave labor more the hallmarks of Nazism than of the Allies fighting Germany? But Goebbels's propaganda did not appeal to reason, only to emotion.

Goebbels went on to declare that only the German Army and German people were strong enough to save Europe from the Bolshevik menace. That was also untrue, as the German defeat at Stalingrad was at that very moment proving. The rest of his speech was an appeal for the German people to sacrifice all to defeat the menace in the East. The climax of his speech came in a series of questions to which the crowd shouted its response, questions such as, did Germans believe in victory, were they ready to do battle, work harder, have total war? Did they have faith in

Hitler? Goebbels concluded with a new slogan in the form of a well-known line from a German poet: "Now, people arise; now, storm, break loose!" *

Goebbels also turned his propaganda machine outward, trying to subvert other European nations, most especially France and Britain. He also beamed, through radio and other means, a great deal of propaganda at the United States. As he had in Germany, Goebbels sought to exploit the fears of Americans. The Great Depression was still in progress. There was a great deal of unemployment. Times were hard. Goebbels blamed these conditions on Jews, Communists, and wealthy "plutocrats." President Roosevelt and other leaders were called "tools" of these "enemies" of the people. Germany was cited as virtuous because it had broken the power of Jews, Communists, and plutocrats and therefore was invincible.

The propaganda had some success in the United States. We stayed out of the war through the fall of Poland, the Low Countries, and France, the Battle of Britain, the enslavement of Greece and the Balkan countries, the invasion of the Soviet Union. Only the attack on Pearl Harbor on December 7, 1941, by the Japanese brought the United States into the war. There were many factors causing America's reluctance to enter the war, but the Goebbels propaganda was intended to keep the United States out of the war, and it succeeded for a time.

Before the war, several organizations, notably the German-American Bund, supported Hitler through publications and rallies. The Nazi salute and its emblem, the swastika, were both seen in America.

Yet, Goebbels's propaganda failed to win Americans to the Nazi cause. Not enough people were convinced. And the fledgling pro-

---

* I am indebted for this analysis of Goebbels's propaganda techniques to Willie A. Boelcke in his introduction to *The Secret Conferences of Dr. Goebbels, The Nazi Propaganda War 1939–43*, which he edited.

Nazi movement disappeared the instant Pearl Harbor was bombed. Goebbels's failure was due in part to the fact he could not control the American press and broadcasting facilities, as he did in Germany. He could not stamp out conflicting information and ideas. Yet, he also failed for reasons suggested by Gordon, Falk, and Hodapp in their book:

> Dr. Goebbels knew the German mind, but the German mind in the 'twenties, 'thirties, and 'forties was decidedly different from the American mind, the British mind and the French mind. And here he committed his cardinal sin as a propagandist: he believed that whatever it was that appealed to the German sense of honor and life values would also appeal to others in different cultures who lived in ways unlike German ways and who prized different things in life and held different kinds of aspirations for their respective futures.

What is the American mind that Goebbels failed to understand? An American is instantly recognized the world over, even when that person tries to adopt the language and ways of his or her host country. Why? What is the American character? Better said, what is it to be an American? And, in the context of this book, if a person (such as Goebbels) wishes to manipulate public opinion in the United States, what basic qualities in an American must that person understand?

It has long been said that it is more difficult to define an American than many other nationalities, such as Englishmen, Frenchmen, Italians, or ethnic groups, such as Arabs, Indians, or Chinese. This difficulty is said to stem from the fact that the United States is such a new country and that Americans consist of so many races and nationalities. Indeed, it is suggested that there is perhaps no such thing as an American, that we are really only transplanted English, Irish, Germans, Blacks, Jews, Slavs, and scores of other racial and ethnic groups.

Undeniably we are the melting pot of nations, yet something happened to all of these peoples who came to this continent, something that made them uniquely American. In searching for that "something" we must begin with the land.

When the first English settlers came to Jamestown in 1607 and to Plymouth in 1620, they found a virgin land, sparsely populated with Indians. The soil was incredibly rich, the resources untapped, the climate temperate. It was a whole continent, full of the riches of the eons. Europe, Asia, Africa, even a large portion of South America, had been heavily populated for thousands of years. The soil, unlike America's, had been deforested, cultivated, grazed, and covered with houses, roads, great cities.

Americans were forever shaped by the land they occupied. Perhaps only Canada and Russia, much of which have a far harsher climate, and Australia share this resource of virgin land awaiting development by the courageous and industrious. Many other lands have the variety of terrain that America has, the mountains and plains, seashores and deserts, lakes and rivers. But few places on earth ever had the billions of acres of incredibly rich soil, glistening with rain and warmed by a temperate sun. There was so much of that soil that Americans, despite their energetic conquest of it, were 300 years populating and tilling it all. And there were so many virgin ores and other resources that despite our at times remorseless plundering of them, we still find 85 percent of our natural resources in this land.

The land has indelibly shaped the American character. For 300 years, American men and women struck out to conquer a succession of new frontiers. Even today, Alaska, called the last frontier, attracts the adventuresome and the dissatisfied. In the last quarter of the twentieth century, we have become a predominantly urban people. No more than 5 percent of our population engages in farming. Yet, the land still holds us, if only a plot of grass in the suburbs or a window box or houseplant in an urban ghetto. Owning and tilling land appeals to people the world over, but nowhere as strongly as in the United States. It is an American characteristic.

The land also shaped Americans because of its primeval majesty.

The beauty of it still survives, even if we have spoiled it in many places. The unspoiled grandeur has inspired the art and literature of America. The land led to a spirit of adventure, to independence, to a feeling of oneness with nature and with God. Above all, the land led Americans, whether early or late settlers, to a feeling of abiding in a special place, especially graced by the divine which made them a special people. For generations, Americans spoke of "manifest destiny" to own and occupy this tremendous empire and to bring their specialness to the world. We have not lost this feeling. All of these qualities are indigenous to Americans, most decidedly the feeling of being special. The land made it so.

Finally, the land made Americans the most profligate wasters the world has ever known. When land on the East Coast wore out from excessive planting of tobacco and cotton, we simply moved westward to fresh land, driving the Indians ahead of us. We felled the trees without number, for there always seemed to be more. We slaughtered animals, sometimes for the sheer joy of killing them, for they seemed without number. We polluted lakes and rivers, for there always seemed to be another one for us to disgorge into. We drained underground lakes of oil, leveled mountains and dug huge craters in the earth to mine the resources, giving no thought that there could ever be any end to the bounty of nature. The American character seems to be forever shaped by the expectation of boundless plenty and the effortless waste of it all.

In 1976, Americans celebrated their 200th year of independence as a nation. Even the earliest settlers do not go back much more than 350 years. As long as that seems, it is rather recent in recorded history. There are buildings in Europe that have been continuously occupied for a thousand years. When Michelangelo sculpted his immortal *Pietà* almost five hundred years ago, he was inspired by that city's peerless Duomo—and the cathedral at Florence is far from the oldest in Europe. Yet, the glories of Europe are recent compared to the antiquities of Greece, the Far East, and

South America. America and Americans are so *new* and that has shaped our character.

It is possible to speculate on how Americans might be different had the first colonists come a century or two earlier. Indeed, the peoples of several South American nations, as well as Mexico, may have a different character, at least in part, because they were colonized a century before the United States. The Spanish, who colonized the lands to the south, brought with them a significantly feudal society. There were classes of people, the concept of nobility with great wealth accumulated from the labor of others, the notion of serfdom dependent upon the largesse of the nobility, and a powerful church to lend morality to it all.

The English, Dutch, Swedish, German, and other early settlers to the United States also had come from feudal societies, but a century had elapsed in Europe and feudalism had waned. The Protestant Reformation, the growth of commerce and the increasing power of merchants, the incipient industrial revolution, the economic failure of feudalism and the breaking up of the great feudal fiefdoms into small farms, the blossoming of art and science, all drastically altered Europe in just a century.

Attempts were made to bring a feudal society of privileged classes to the United States, but it didn't work. Captain John Smith complained of the "gentlemen" who contributed no work to his fledgling colony. The land, the colder climate, particularly in New England, the hostile Indians, made this country an inhospitable place for the idle and lazy. Throughout the Colonial period, various English governors tried to impose the trappings of the royal court. They succeeded from time to time, yet the trappings were always terribly out of place. One of the aims of the revolution was to get rid of them.

The absence of a feudal background is a key to understanding the American character. Our forefathers may not have had a classless society, but they were anything but feudal. The idea of privileged classes was abhorrent to them. Benjamin Franklin wore a homespun suit amid the silks and satins of the courts at Paris and London. The Constitution expressly forbids the use of titles of nobility and the acceptance of gifts by public officials. In the 1830s, the farmers of Appalachia rebelled at the ballot box and "threw the rascals" of the "Virginia Dynasty" out of the White House. In electing Andrew Jackson, whom they considered one of their own, the frontier people were rejecting the idea of privilege and hereditary classes. During our bloody decades (from approximately 1870 to 1930) of labor violence, American workmen were striking and dying in defense of the notion that they were not a subservient class and had a right to participate in the decisions and share the wealth of the industrialists. Blacks, Indians, the poor, and women still fight similar battles. The idea of an egalitarian society is deeply ingrained in the American character. We have trouble when we depart very far from it.

A companion to equality has been the idea of opportunity. Those frontiersmen in Jackson's day, the bloodied strikers at the turn of this century, today's Blacks, Indians, poor, and women demanding equal rights, have not and are not seeking to take away the rights and wealth of others, but only to garner them for themselves. Americans have not particularly attacked wealth or even disliked it. On the contrary we have long adored wealth—so much so that the idea is for everyone to have it. Such ideas as socialism and communism, the notion of distributing wealth, have been mostly rejected in America.

The idea of equal opportunity is integral to the American character. The Puritans came for the opportunity to worship as they pleased and to prosper. The proprietary Colonies, such as Maryland, were founded by men seeking a fortune. The seemingly boundless land to the west beckoned to generations of dissatisfied Americans and to wave upon wave of immigrants. The frontier people suffered privation, hard work, and an early death because they believed in the opportunity at hand. Even in an industrialized and urban America, we believe that opportunity lies in a small business, perhaps, or a new product or technique, or some literary or artistic achievement, or through education. The expectation of opportunity to fulfill personal ambitions, while not unique to the United States, is at the core of nearly every American mind.

Underlying the egalitarian society and the idea of opportunity —indeed, what made them possible—was the idea of freedom. The earliest settler sought it, if only in terms of religious freedom and then, in the case of the Puritans, interpreted it as freedom to burn witches and discriminate against other religions. But the germ of freedom fell on fertile soil and prospered. The land and the frontier made it so. For a long time, dissenters and seekers of liberty could find a virgin spot to exercise it. The founders of the nation wrote the concepts of liberty into our most hallowed documents, the Declaration of Independence, the Constitution, and the Bill of Rights.

Critics detect a hollow ring to the bell of liberty. Our long subjugation and oppression of Blacks and Indians is impossible to square with our ideals of liberty. Our periods of discrimination against Jews and a number of ethnic minorities confront our ideals. Our economic discrimination that has led to chronic poverty in a land of plenty seems the opposite of freedom of opportunity. The various times in which we have sought to smother dissent, our unsavory history of political trials, and our demogogic witchhunts for suspected un-Americans led to more embarrassment than pride.

Yet, if our performance has at times been poor, the ideal has always been there. It beckoned millions of immigrants for almost a century. In the 1960s, it again beckoned a new wave of foreign-born to our shores and continues in the 1970s. The ideal of freedom has been of incalculable value to Americans and shaped our character. Imperfect as it may be, the liberty of Americans is among the greatest in the world. The ideal has shaped our political system and our court system. It has helped to extend the vote. It has permitted us many times to correct the abuses of liberty. It has given every American a goal, a birthright, something to believe in and strive for.

There are a number of other qualities that can be cited as rather typically American: a basic optimism that is often irrepressible; an openness, expansiveness, lack of guile, and distrust of secrecy; friendliness, charitableness, and neighborliness toward others in need of help; a "can do" attitude of surmounting obstacles and a competitiveness in winning, and hating to lose; a need for quick results and impatience with the long drawn out; a worshiping of bigness; a penchant for instant enthusiasms and fads—and a just as instant discarding of them; a fascination with gadgets and things mechanical and technological; a pronounced streak of violence and some fascination with it; and, again for emphasis, a conviction that to be an American is somehow to be chosen, to be endowed with some special wisdom and ability.

Many, many will disagree with this analysis of the American character—and probably rightly so. It is extremely difficult to define Americans. We are such a racial and ethnic mixture, so individualistic in our attitudes. Yet there clearly is an American character. A person need only live abroad for a period of time to realize the uniqueness of being an American, although that realization doesn't make it any easier to describe our national characteristics.

However a person defines an American, the point is that the way we think, both individually and collectively, has at least some characteristics different and even unique from other nationalities. We have been shaped by this land, our climate, our experiences as a people. Anyone who would manipulate public opinion in the United States must be reasonably successful in understanding the American character and appealing to it. Fortunately for us and the world, the diabolical Dr. Goebbels failed in that task.

CHAPTER THREE Is Education Propaganda?

When a revolutionary government assumes power in a nation, among its first acts is to seize the radio and television broadcasting stations and to close and censor the press. These actions are attempts to mold public opinion behind the regime by controlling the sources of information the people have.

Another early step is to close the nation's schools. They are reopened a few days later with new or censored textbooks and new teachers loyal to the regime and its philosophy. Education is a primary source of information, an important molder of public opinion. Any revolutionary government, particularly a totalitarian one, wants its citizens thoroughly indoctrinated with a particular view of the nation's history, the causes of the revolution, and a favorable attitude toward the revolution. Communist governments are particularly energetic in taking over the educational process. As Communists took over South Vietnam and Cambodia in 1975, they quickly set up indoctrination or "reeducation" sessions for citizens. Such meetings are routine in the People's Republic of China. Attendance is compulsory.

Such abuse of the education system is anathema to Americans. Intellectual freedom, that is, the ability of a teacher or professor to say and write nearly anything he or she believes to be true, is as important in the United States as freedom of speech and freedom of the press.

Still, the American system of education molds public attitudes. We think as we do in large measure because of the education we receive in school. Even though we may have forgotten much of the specific information learned in school, our attitudes toward

America and Americans are rooted in one way or another in what we learned in school as a child.* We may have received a good education or a poor one. We may have developed a lifelong love of learning or a distaste for study. We may or may not have developed the ability to think critically for ourselves. Our schooling may have led to a vocation or profession. But it is far more certain that our core of knowledge about American history and the American form of government was learned in school at an early age.

The study of history has long been maligned. Henry Ford, the auto magnate, said, "History is bunk." He was merely echoing an even more caustic comment by Napoleon Bonaparte of France: "What is history but a fable agreed upon?"

Such comments are probably unduly cynical and unfair. The American philosopher George Santayana may have been more accurate with the statement: "Those who cannot remember the past are condemned to repeat it." Yet, there is a little bunk to history, and some of what is written is more likely fable than fact. Few really believe anymore that George Washington cut down a cherry tree and said he could not tell a lie when confronted by his father. The much-told tale of the Pilgrims and Indians sitting down to the first Thanksgiving cannot erase the evidence of brutal relations between the groups. One of Captain Myles Standish's first acts was to raid the Indian burial grounds to rob graves of the ceremonial grain buried there. After several skirmishes, Standish invited the Indian chief, his eighteen-year-old son, and two other braves to his headquarters for a feast. Once inside, the door was locked. Standish personally hacked one Indian to death with his

---

* I am not attempting in this chapter any form of critique of American education. Nor am I seeking to give a history of it. The intention is to make readers aware of some of the effects of education on public opinion. No judgment is made about whether these effects are good or ill.

knife, while other Pilgrims dispatched the two Indian braves. The chief's son was spared long enough to be taken outside and hanged as an example. The Thanksgiving story, with its charming image of friendship between the Indians and Pilgrims, is more fable than fact.

A certain amount of legend creeps into history. Even when historians are highly disciplined about sticking to the facts of the past, they have great difficulty discerning fact from fable or learning all the facts. In re-creating the facts, a historian studies old records and official documents, newspaper accounts, published reports, and biographies of participants. If the event is of more recent origin, he can perhaps interview participants. Yet, try as they will, historians can never gain a completely accurate knowledge of a past event. No one knows this more than a historian. Repeated studies may show a particular account of the past to be accurate on the facts as known, but this history may change if new facts develop.

History, as reported by historians, also has a point of view. This is probably inescapable, and the facts of history are thereby changed. An Indian view of early American history might speak of invasion of their lands by white Europeans, expropriation of historical tribal lands, Indian kindnesses and generosity toward settlers, which was rewarded with treachery, broken promises, and brutality. Indian history might also speak of forced marches and relocations of whole tribes and nations, failure to extend basic American rights to Indians, prejudice ("The only good Indian is a dead Indian"), more and more broken treaties, and the decades of Indian wars in which Indians fought with incredible valor.

In recent years, schools and colleges in the United States have begun to teach what is frequently called black history. It attempts to recognize the long history (Blacks were among the earliest explorers, and the first slaves arrived a year before the Pilgrims) of black people on these shores. History attempts to recognize the many contributions of Blacks to America, as well as the long, dreadful history of slavery and oppression and its effects on Americans of all races.

There are many other views of history. The British view of the American Revolution is somewhat different from that taught in the United States. There is a Catholic view of history, particularly the Reformation period, which varies in important ways from that conceived by Protestants. Similarly, there is a Jewish view of history and a Moslem and Hindu and Buddhist. Every nationality has a conception of historical events that varies from every other nation's. The Spanish, for example, are very proud of the centuries in which they dominated much of the world. Even today they cite the influence of the Spanish language throughout the world. Here in the United States there is a Southern view of history, particularly the Civil War era, which many Yankees disagree with. Westerners tend to approach historical matters from a different point of view than Easterners.

The point is not that one view is "right" and the other "wrong." Even if all the facts of history could be learned, the result would hardly be "truth." Every fact, every event, is open to interpretation. When Patrick Henry said, "Give me liberty or give me death," was he being a firebrand unwilling to compromise, or a patriot defending freedom? When Chicago police opened fire on protestors at Haymarket Square in 1886 and a riot broke out, were they maintaining law and order, or squashing peaceful dissent with violent oppression? When President Ford vetoed a housing bill in 1975, was he maintaining the nation's fiscal integrity, as he said, or failing to help ill-housed citizens, as his Congressional opponents suggested? Historians of the future may not have to decide which point of view is "true," but their reporting of the veto may help to color the thinking of those who read them. That both views or all views may be correct is not always easy to write into history texts.

An American view of history has been taught in public schools for generations. Indeed, the repeated study of American history is compulsory.* This learned view of history is an important reason why we think as we do.

If we try as hard as we can to avoid making judgments on whether the learned view is right or wrong, correct or incorrect, we can still observe some of the ways the teaching of American history affects public opinion. For starters, there is an inevitable tendency to inflate the United States's role in world affairs. American history is generally taught separately from world history, which is not as compulsory a subject. Americans tend to know more American history than world history. Many of the important events of American history, such as the settlement of the West, the various wars, the industrialization of the nation, went relatively unnoticed in world events of the time. The United States did not become a powerful force in world affairs until its entry into World War I in 1917. It did not become a world leader until World War II in 1941. The emphasis on American events tends to give a person a distorted view of the historical importance of the United States.

There is also a tendency—likewise probably inevitable—to present past events in the most favorable light and to glorify the nation's leaders as heroes. Every nation does this. It seems to have value in inculcating pride and patriotism. Portraits are drawn, statues erected, monuments constructed, streets and buildings named for heroes. Despite our egalitarian principles, we Americans also honor our great and near great. The inspiring monuments to Washington, Lincoln, and Jefferson in the nation's capital are shrines visited by millions of citizens each year. The largest sculptures in the world are at Mount Rushmore, South Dakota, where

---

* Students receive an introduction to American history in the early grades, then a more formal course in the fourth, fifth, or sixth grade. The subject is taught again in junior high school and once more in senior high school. One reason for the much-observed boredom of many students with history may be simply that the same basic information is taught too often.

the likenesses of Washington, Jefferson, Lincoln, and Theodore Roosevelt are carved in stone as giants. In a reaction to the tragic assassination of President John F. Kennedy in 1963, a space center, a leading international airport, scores of streets and buildings, were renamed in his honor, and a new cultural center bears his name.

The glorification of a president or another leader certainly has the advantage of inculcating pride and patriotism, yet there are drawbacks, which historians have begun to point out in recent years. By its nature, the process of glorifying a person means concentrating on his virtues, triumphs, and successes, while choosing to ignore his weaknesses and failures. To give one example: Lincoln is revered for emancipating the slaves, his determination to save the union of the states, his compassion for people, his eloquence in stating the aspirations of the nation in simple terms, the dignity and humaneness of his personality. Yet, many historians criticize Lincoln for freeing the slaves too late and in a halfhearted fashion. He freed the slaves only in the Confederate states, where he had no power to enforce his proclamation, not in the Union states. He is also criticized for greatly extending presidential power, often conducting the war without the approval of Congress or legal authority. He also authorized the abrogation of many civil rights in America, leading to the arrest of thousands of his critics. It has been said he had compassion for individuals and small groups of people, yet allowed his generals to conduct the war so as to cause great and probably needless casualties. As all men, Lincoln was a compendium of virtues and faults, wisdom and expediency. The glorification of Lincoln as a national hero simply makes it more difficult to criticize him and to present a balanced view of his administration.

Perhaps more serious is the charge, made by many historians in recent years, that the glorification of so-called "strong" presidents has altered the office of president and our form of government. For many years, historians have played a game of ranking presidents in some fashion such as great, near great, average, weak, and poor. In general, the "great" presidents have been those who made historic decisions, presided over important events—usually a war—and enhanced the power of the presidency at the expense of Congress, the courts, the states, and the people. The great or strong presidents generally include Washington, Jefferson, Jackson, Lincoln, Theodore Roosevelt, Wilson, Franklin Roosevelt, and Truman. Presidents who presided in more tranquil times or who saw their duty as sharing power with Congress, or sought not to aggrandize power for their office, are generally not so highly regarded by historians.*

A reaction to this ranking game began to occur in the 1960s. As historians and political scientists became concerned about the growth of presidential powers, particularly war powers, they began to wonder if the glorification of strong presidents and the ranking game was not pushing presidents to assume ever greater powers and prerogatives. There seemed to be no shortage of examples. The war in Vietnam, conducted by several presidents, notably Lyndon Johnson and Richard Nixon, seemed to go on by White House decree with Congress powerless to stop it. American armed forces were being used in various places in the world as presidents saw fit. In domestic matters, presidents were assuming the right to impound, that is, not spend money legally appropriated by Congress. During the Watergate affair President Nixon sought to cloak all of his activities and those of his associates, past and present, in the principle of executive privilege. He contended that no report had to be made to Congress, the courts, or the people.

A number of scholars began to blame themselves and their colleagues for encouraging the growth of presidential powers by perhaps excessive praise of war presidents. Political scientist Robert J. Bresler wrote in the *Nation* in 1970:

* For a fuller treatment read the author's *Presidential Power: How Much Is Too Much?* (McGraw-Hill Inc., New York, 1972) and *Defense Against Tyranny* (Julian Messner, New York, 1975).

Americans, especially liberals, should be embarrassed to recall, as Richard Neustadt, author of *Presidential Power*, has acknowledged, that they helped to create the myth which so loosely equated presidential greatness with the exercise of war powers. . . . Great presidents would have to be strong presidents, and for liberals it was no more than coincidence that strong presidents invariably became war presidents.

Nor was it just war powers that led to criticism. Many people in and out of government expressed fears about the growth of the power of the federal bureaucracy to regulate nearly every aspect of American life: the possibility of abuse by law-enforcement agencies, such as the Federal Bureau of Investigation, the Central Intelligence Agency, and the Internal Revenue Service; excessive governmental secrecy; and the growth of what President Eisenhower called the "military-industrial complex."

Many factors led to the growth of the power of the White House and the executive branch of government, but one of the causes may well have been the glorification of presidents in history texts. Modal American public opinion came to accept the desirability of having strong presidents who went to war and increased executive power, in part because of the educational process that glorified such presidents over the so-called "weak" presidents. The history texts did not have to be written that way. For example, in the very serious depression of 1873, President Grant was asked what his program was to combat it. He replied that he had no program because it was up to Congress to prepare and legislate such a program. Historians could have praised Grant for abiding by the Constitution and its doctrine of separation of powers between the legislative and executive branches. Instead, he has been scorned as among our "weakest" presidents. Thus, the writing and teaching of history influenced the way Americans think about presidents and encouraged the growth of presidential power.

Many charges have been made over the years that American history, as taught in schools, tends to distort the history and thus the opinion Americans have of themselves. A great deal of effort has been made by historians and publishers of textbooks to offset these criticisms and achieve a more balanced view of American history. Much progress has been made. Again, without making a judgment of whether these criticisms are valid, we can consider some of them.

We have already encountered a major one, the charge that for too long only white history was taught in schools. The history of black citizens and their contributions to America were ignored. A similar criticism is made concerning Indians. It is said that our often disreputable treatment of the native population should be reported. Women's organizations are contending that the role of women and the search for women's rights has not been accurately covered. They argue that American history is often male history and thereby sexist oriented. Various ethnic and religious minorities also feel neglected in history texts. The charge is made that for too long American history has been the history of white, Anglo-Saxon, Protestant males. A different history could have led to greater appreciation and understanding of the role and importance of minorities in America.

Another frequent criticism is that American wars tend to be glorified and that not enough history of the opposition to the wars is reported. Every American war, except World War II, met with vocal, sometimes violent, opposition. Many Americans were opposed to the Revolution on the grounds that Americans were British citizens and should remain loyal to the Crown. The grievances against the London government did not seem serious enough to warrant the bloodshed. The War of 1812 was bitterly opposed. New England states threatened to secede from the union. Critics felt it an evil for the United States to support the despot Napoleon against the British.

The Mexican war aroused furious opposition because it was conceived as an open seizure of Mexican lands to extend slavery into the West. The Civil War met vociferous opposition from both

Southern sympathizers living in the North and from those who felt it was wrong for brother to fight brother. Opponents believed the slavery and other issues could have been resolved without war. So great was the opposition that Lincoln, a Republican, had to suspend civil liberties and accept a so-called "war Democrat," Andrew Johnson, as his running mate in 1864.

The Spanish American War and particularly the Philippine Insurrection which followed it were seen by opponents as an example of American imperialism to gain overseas colonies. World War I was opposed by many labor groups who felt that the United States was supporting capitalism, by pro-German groups, and by many who felt the United States should stay out of a purely European conflict. Some historians believe that if the United States had stayed out of the war, it would have been settled by negotiation, drastically altering the history of the world and probably preventing World War II.

There was relatively little opposition to the Second World War. The Japanese had attacked Hawaii, an American possession. Nazi Germany under Adolf Hitler was perceived as a menace to be eradicated at any cost. Yet, there had been great opposition to entry into the war prior to the attack on Pearl Harbor by the Japanese. The Korean War, beginning in 1950, eventually gained considerable opposition from citizens who did not believe in President Truman's concept of a "limited war." Some persons believed the United States should use all its resources to destroy North Korea and mainland China. The war in Vietnam began to arouse massive opposition in the late 1960s from citizens who felt the conflict was morally and legally wrong.

All of these wars went on. There were justifications for the wars and they were supported by prevailing public opinion. The point being made is not that the wars were right or wrong, but that failure to report the opposition to the wars distorts reality. Many Americans, remembering only World War II, were surprised and frightened by the mass demonstrations and violence of the Vietnam War protests. Actually, the protests were fairly routine for American wars and rather tame compared to those of the past. It is argued that a more balanced view of history would have led to a greater understanding of both America's tendency to go to war and of the reasons for opposition to it.

When the United States finally pulled out of Southeast Asia, and South Vietnam and Cambodia were lost to the Communists, many commentators and newspapermen, perhaps reflecting public attitudes, cited the Vietnam War as the first Americans had ever "lost." This may well be the case, but it is at least arguable that American military success is a bit exaggerated. In both the Revolution and the War of 1812 we were dependent upon French help to defeat a rather small force of British troops. In the Mexican War we defeated, with some difficulty, the forces of an impoverished and politically divided nation. A similar statement can be made about the Spanish-American War. In World War I and II we were allied with some of the most powerful military forces in the world. The Korean War came to a negotiated cease-fire following a stalemate. The war never officially began or ended, and American troops are still there nearly a quarter century after the fighting stopped. That America's fighting men have been valorous and often victorious should not necessarily lead to a conclusion of invincibility. An awareness of the defeat, struggles, and futilities of America's wars might lead to a different view of America by Americans. Our way of thinking about war, whether that be right or wrong, is in part a product of the educational process. If the teaching were different, our thinking would be different.

Authors of history texts devote generous space to the industrialization of America. A difficult period in our history, filled with controversy at the time and ever since, it was more than just a period of railroad building and factory construction. It was a time when many of America's great corporations were built, often at the cost of smothering and destroying nearly all competitors by practices that were shoddy, shady, corrupt, and sometimes brutal.

More, the years from the 1870s into the 1930s were years of terrible labor violence. Company guards, police, national guardsmen, and even federal troops, opened fire repeatedly on strikers. There were strikes that resembled open warfare. Deaths by the dozen and score in a single fusillade of gunfire were common. It was an unhappy era in American history. A desire to forget these unsavory events ought not lead to a conception of Americans as peaceful, reasonable citizens marching along a road of orderly progress. Again, the way we were taught, both in what we learned and were not given a chance to learn, influenced the way we think today. Different information, a different emphasis, could have led to a different way of thinking about ourselves and our economic system.

There is much about the history of the American people that is ennobling—the courage of the pioneers and frontier settlers, the patriotism of soldiers and civilians, the generosity of spirit that often makes Americans the most charitable people in the world, the inventiveness and industriousness, the openness and friendliness, the individuality that is almost a birthmark. Yet, there is a strain of surprising violence, the picket-line massacres, the vigilantes taking the law into their own hands, the night riders, the lynch mob, gunmen and robbers and organized criminals, the bootleggers of the Prohibition period in the 1920s, the repeated graft and corruption of government officials at all levels. America's history may be short, as history goes in some nations, but it is surely a colorful one. Ours is a young, rambunctious nation. We never did anything by halves. We gave liberty to our citizens and have paid a bit of a penalty in the form of crime, violence, and being rather unloving toward one's neighbor.

There are those who maintain—and perhaps properly so—that the negative aspects of American history should not be taught, especially to young children. A popular bumper sticker reads: AMERICA: LOVE HER OR LEAVE HER. That slogan is open to several interpretations. Most people are critical from time to time of parents, children, wives, and others they love the most. They are not about to leave them. Yet, to some people the slogan suggests that America is right whatever it (or she) does and that it is unpatriotic to criticize any action of the government.

It is also argued that it is important and valuable for school children to develop a sense of patriotism. This can be done best, it is maintained, by teaching respect for the nation, its past and its leaders, and by textbooks that honor the best that we have done, Emphasizing past mistakes serves no useful purpose. It is better to concentrate on accomplishments and virtues so that children may learn to emulate these.

These views are widely held. Many organized groups believe it is their job to see that a mostly, sometimes entirely, favorable view of the events of American history is taught in schools. Textbook writers and teachers feel a pressure to present a view of America that is acceptable to what are often called "patriotic" groups.

There is another view suggesting (with Santayana) that not knowing the mistakes of our past, we are condemned to repeat them. Even a cursory study of picket-line massacres, civil rights protests, and dissent to America's wars indicates that violence occurs when there is a confrontation between police or soldiers and pickets or protestors. When police keep their guns holstered and the protest is allowed to proceed in a peaceful manner, then violence is generally avoided. In May 1970, Ohio National Guardsmen opened fire on students at Kent State University who were protesting the American invasion of Cambodia. Four were killed. If the guardsmen and their officers had had even elementary knowledge of the many similar massacres of the past, they would not have loaded their weapons or perhaps even carried them. But the soldiers did not know this history and the tragedy unfolded.

A realistic view of our past may help us understand how the United States has gone to war and why it remained at peace; when intervention in foreign affairs has been beneficial and why we have become entangled in problems not of our own making; why our economic system functions well and why it plunges into depression or soars into an inflationary spiral; and perhaps most importantly how this nation and its people have changed over the 200 years of independence.

Knowledge of the unpleasant and distasteful in our past, rather than fostering disrespect, can encourage pride. The lawlessness of the wild West is a fact, and a student can admire the struggles of frontier people to bring law and order to their settlements. Displacement and destruction of our Indian population is a fact. Modern Americans can admire the resistance of the Indians and their efforts to maintain their own identity. Night riders and lynch mobs preying on black people for centuries is a fact. All Americans can take pride that Blacks both resisted and prevailed over evil.

An honest presentation of American history, rather than a glorified one, can lead to an appreciation of how far we have come in taming ourselves as well as this land we inhabit. An example is the somewhat popular theme of recent years that Americans are a violent people. Many Americans became concerned about this during the civil rights protests of the 1950s, the ghetto riots and bombings of the 1960s, the mass arrests of Vietnam protestors, and the bombings of public buildings, as well as the seemingly great rise in street crime. A presidential commission was appointed to study the causes of violence in America. A number of books were written to analyze our violent natures. The subject began to be taught in schools in the hope that children could be weaned away from violence.

The simple facts are that we are a far, far less violent people than we used to be. The evidence is overwhelming, although many people find it difficult to believe. We have become almost pacific in terms of Indian massacres, religious riots, ethnic mob actions, racial lynchings, and labor violence, all of which marred our history for generations and have greatly decreased if not entirely disappeared. Perhaps only in crime has violence increased and even that is open to dispute. We simply do not have records of how much crime occurred in Colonial times or even the last century. Today we have abundant records of reported crime. We have no way of knowing whether we have more or less murders, robberies, and assaults than in the past, although any of it is too much.

It is arguable that we Americans should not be afraid of our past, that we can take pride both in our accomplishments and in our growing maturity as a people, that we can continue to learn from our mistakes. Certainly, one of the best defenses a people can have against propaganda is an educational system devoted to the truth.

Is education propaganda? Clearly, yes. The totalitarian nations seek to rigidly control the educational process and thus the minds of their citizens. In the United States, our guarantees of freedoms of speech and press, our tradition of intellectual freedom, preclude this sort of rigid governmental interference, although many a school board and school administrator has tried (and succeeded sometimes) to control and censor what is being taught. Perhaps every teacher has felt at least once in a while frustration and fear in attempting to impart information and ideas that are unpopular. A young teacher can lose his or her job for delving into controversial matters too forthrightly. This tends to make education lean toward the conservative and safe, teaching that which upholds prevailing public opinion, neglecting that which might alter it.

As this chapter has tried to show, those who write and publish history texts feel a compulsion to write a view of history that is conservative and safe, so that the book may have as wide a sale as possible. By their very nature, all such books must have a point of view and select from a myriad of facts those that support the viewpoint, ignoring or downplaying those that oppose it.

It is perhaps inevitable, therefore, that education, as the primary source of historical information, greatly influences the way we think about our nation, our government, and our problems. It is likewise probably inevitable that education be propaganda. Yet, we could strive toward a goal of making the information taught in school more impartial, offering the information that would sustain other, even conflicting, points of view.

CHAPTER FOUR   The Lethal Role of Secrecy

On January 8, 1918, President Woodrow Wilson went before Congress to announce his famous Fourteen Points for making World War I "the war to end all wars." The first of his points is the most celebrated: "Open covenants openly arrived at."

This seemed terribly naive and idealistic to European statesmen, particularly when Wilson went on to urge freedom of the seas, free trade between nations, disarmament, adjustment of colonial claims, and creation of several new nations in Europe on the basis of what later came to be called self-determination of peoples. Georges Clemenceau, the premier of France, scoffed at the Fourteen Points, saying "even God Almighty has only ten!"—a reference to the Ten Commandments of the Bible.

When Wilson suggested "open covenants openly arrived at" he was advocating nonsecret diplomacy. The diplomats of the world should meet, their deliberations open to public scrutiny, and arrange a peace the people of the world knew about and could support. There should be no secret deals, no territorial grabs, which indeed had already been secretly negotiated among the European powers. Wilson knew what he was suggesting was idealistic. In a speech in Sioux Falls, South Dakota, on September 8, 1919, he said: "Sometimes people call me an idealist. Well, that is the way I know I am an American. America is the only idealistic nation in the world."

America was idealistic then. In entering World War I, abrogating our long fear of foreign entanglements, which George Washington in his Farewell Address had urged Americans to avoid, we were "making the world safe for democracy." The bell of liberty never pealed more clearly. The principles of the American Revolution, self-determination for free people to rule themselves, never had a better advocacy. And, when Wilson went to Europe to seek those elusive "open covenants," he was welcomed by jubilant and adoring crowds who saw him and the United States as the symbol of liberty.

Wilson did not prevail. He attended the peace conference, but could not prevent the secret deals and the harsh terms that set the stage for World War II in 1939. He was successful in having several new nations created in Europe, the Balkan states, Austria, Hungary, Czechoslovakia, an independent Poland, the Baltic states of Latvia, Lithuania, and Estonia. The achievement in which he took the most pride was creation of the League of Nations, a beginning of world government. Wilson's dreams were shattered when Congress failed to ratify either the peace treaty or to join the League of Nations. America retreated into isolationism, not emerging as a full participant in world affairs until 1940.

The word "open" was important to Americans in those days. Wilson used it twice in five words in the Fourteen Points. In 1899, the United States espoused the "open door" policy toward China. It sought to leave China open to free trade by all nations, although some feel the term really disguised American imperialism. Whether or not that was true, the American people saw theirs as an open society. In a democracy, everything should be known to the people so they could govern themselves. Everyone should be treated evenhandedly. Idealism was a worthy goal. Lying and deception were denounced. At least in stating the principles of openness and idealism, Wilson probably spoke for the majority of the American people.

These ideals died hard in America, if indeed they have or can ever entirely expire. Some steps toward their demise are: In World War II, Americans became accustomed to the need to protect defense secrets. Weather reports went off the radio; they might give information in case the Germans or Japanese wanted to bomb us.

Defense plants and public buildings were plastered with posters warning against loose talk, which enemy agents might overhear. The Norden bombsight that permitted accurate daylight bombing was an important secret. Americans were proud of the device and of its secrecy.

The nation's greatest secret of the war was the Manhattan Project, which developed the atomic bomb. Americans understood the need for the secrecy. When the doomsday weapon was exploded over Japan, Americans instinctively felt that such an awesome weapon was better kept entirely in American hands. Other nations should not be tempted to have such a means of destruction. We were distraught when the Russians stole the atomic secrets and built their own bomb. We insisted on full and open inspection of each nation's weapons and atomic facilities. When the Soviet Union refused this principle, we considered it proof of their bad faith. More than ever, the Soviet Union was perceived as a threat to America and world peace.

As World War II drew to a close, Presidents Roosevelt and Truman held much-publicized meetings with the leaders of our wartime allies, Britain and the Soviet Union. Most Americans understood that Wilson's principles of open covenants openly arrived at had not worked—but only because other nations did not have open societies. The presidents were granted tacit approval to negotiate secretly with the Soviets and British. Yet, there was also a tacit understanding that the secrecy afforded Mr. Roosevelt and Mr. Truman was simply a negotiating convenience. Americans clearly believed that the presidents would not reach any agreement that could not be revealed to the American people. In effect, we were engaging in secret diplomacy as an aid to cooperating with the British and Russians, not because we wanted to.

In the late 1940s and through the 1950s and 1960s, most American leaders and the majority of citizens perceived the Soviet Union and the People's Republic of China, as well as most other communist nations, as a threat to peace, freedom, and the United States.

Americans feared Soviet and Chinese expansionism—they would use any means to destroy free, democratic governments, including use of military force. We believed that even the United States was so threatened. Americans saw that they had a need and a duty to oppose communism as an ideology and Soviet and Chinese expansionism.

The confrontation between democracy and communism—the United States and the Soviet Union—came to be known as the "cold war." There was some actual fighting in Korea and Vietnam, but American and Russian troops seldom if ever engaged one another. The cold war meant unrelenting antipathy, gross mistrust, and colossal preparations for wars in the belief that gigantic armaments would prevent the other from attacking.

The very term, cold war, meant that the United States Government maintained in place many of the practices that had seemed essential during World War II. Defense secrets had to be protected. A large intelligence apparatus had to be maintained to spy on the enemy. Secret diplomacy leading to secret deals, once denounced by America, was approved as a necessity in fighting the worldwide communist menace.

The American people, long accustomed to an open government that they believed dealt honestly with them, were asked in the name of the cold war to become used to widespread secrecy in government, secret diplomacy, deception by government officials, and even open lies. This was a major change in the American form of government and a traumatic experience for Americans.

There are a number of known examples of deception and/or lies. Here are a few:

1) In 1961, Adlai Stevenson, American Ambassador to the United Nations, stood in the world body to denounce as lies a charge by Cuba that American planes had participated in the invasion of Cuba at the Bay of Pigs. A few days later the Cuban charge was admitted to be true.

2) In 1964, President Lyndon B. Johnson announced that North

Vietnamese torpedo boats had attacked two American destroyers in the Gulf of Tonkin off Vietnam. The destroyers were described as making an innocent passage on the high seas. The attack was called unprovoked. Congress, reacting to the attack, authorized Mr. Johnson to take all necessary steps to "repel any armed attack against the forces of the United States and to prevent further aggression." For years, the Gulf of Tonkin Resolution was interpreted as Congressional authorization for the war in Vietnam. Later, it was learned that the American destroyers were supporting a raid by South Vietnamese forces on North Vietnamese territory. The "attack" on the American ships was a defensive action by the North Vietnamese.

3) In 1965, President Johnson sent American forces into the Dominican Republic, he said, to prevent a communist takeover and to save the lives of Americans. He said the American Embassy was under attack and that the ambassador had talked to him while hiding under a desk to escape bullets whizzing over his head. Reporters at the scene could find few known Communists amid the Dominican rebels and no evidence of an attack on the American Embassy.

4) In 1968, President Johnson declared the war in Vietnam about over. In reply, the North Vietnamese launched the famous Tet offensive, sending American and South Vietnamese forces reeling. This was but one of many similar instances in which favorable reports on the progress of the war turned out to be false.

5) In 1969 and 1970, President Nixon authorized more than 2,600 bombing raids on Cambodia, a neutral Southeast Asian nation. Not only were the raids kept secret, military and other records were falsified to conceal that the raids took place.

6) For more than two years following the Watergate burglary in June 1972, President Nixon and his associates consistently lied to the American people about the burglary and the investigation of it. When Mr. Nixon's lies were ultimately proven, he resigned from office.

To repeat, these and many other examples of deception and deceit were traumatic experiences for Americans. Lying is still considered grossly immoral in America. Some Americans defended at the time, and still do, the need for the deceptions. In this view, the United States is at war. The ends of democracy justify deceitful means.

Others were appalled by the lies. In January 1969, a subcommittee of the Senate Foreign Relations Committee concluded an exhaustive study of American commitments to foreign nations. It repeatedly found many secret agreements and military commitments, made by various presidents, which had been unknown to Congress or the people. In referring to one, a deal for the United States to pay secretly the cost of Thailand troops fighting in Vietnam, the subcommittee wrote:

> This was pure deception, and it is one of the worst offenses a supposedly free and democratic government can commit against its own people, because it tends to destroy that trust which is an indispensable element of self-government.

In a half century, Americans had receded from the principle of "open covenants openly arrived at" to secret deals, secret bombings, secret invasions concealed by half-truths and lies. The deceit led to a classic situation of liars, the need for more lies to cover old lies—and to gross distrust of all statements.

This situation has an effect—a devastating one—on why we think as we do. Events are important molders of public opinion, particularly if widely known and experienced firsthand. An example would be a natural disaster, such as a tornado or hurricane, flood or famine. Even man-made disasters, such as an explosion and fire, the famous East Coast blackout of 1965, an economic depression with widespread unemployment, can instantly gel public attitudes.

Other events can have the same effect. The Japanese attack on Pearl Harbor is a classic example. Virtually to a person, Americans reacted with outrage, fear, and patriotic fervor. America had been attacked. Great damage had been inflicted with much loss of life. The West Coast seemed in peril of an immediate attack or invasion. Within minutes, men rushed to enlist in the armed forces to defend the nation. Some scientists have called such a reaction instinctive in human beings, an example of the territorial imperative, an animal instinct to defend one's territory from intruders.

Many, many events have cemented public opinion among Americans. A few come quickly to mind. When the atmoic bomb was dropped on Hiroshima and Nagasaki in 1945—a total surprise—Americans reacted with what might be described as pride in the national achievement, relief that the war could be ended quickly, and mostly fear that the future would be forever changed by this weapon.

When the Soviet Union "liberated" and then enslaved the eastern European nations under communist yoke in 1945, Americans were disappointed, outraged, and then fearful of a new menace to world peace.

When North Korea invaded South Korea in 1950, Americans reacted with a determination to repel aggression anywhere in the world.

When the Russians were the first to launch a satellite in orbit of the earth in 1957 and later were the first to put a man in space, Americans reacted with fear, but mostly with chagrin that Soviet technology exceeded ours. A tremendous competitiveness arose. Americans became determined to catch up with and exceed the Russians in space exploration.

In the late 1950s and early 1960s, Americans reacted with outrage and embarrassment to televised scenes of peaceful civil rights marchers kneeling in prayer while mounted troopers attacked them with bullwhips and chains.

The assassinations of President John F. Kennedy, Senator Robert F. Kennedy, and Dr. Martin Luther King, Jr., as well as the maiming of Governor George C. Wallace of Alabama, all occurring between 1963 and 1972, shocked Americans and led to concerns about national violence.

If events have such a powerful effect on public opinion, what happens when secrecy, deception, and lies intervene to create what might be called "nonevents"? Consider the many bombing raids on Cambodia in 1969 and 1970. The American people did not know of these raids on a supposedly neutral nation until 1974. In the absence of knowledge, no public opinion could develop concerning the bombing.

Yet, the bombing and the secrecy had an indirect effect on American public opinion of considerable importance. It is impossible to bomb in secret. The Cambodians surely knew they were being bombed and by whom. The South Vietnamese knew and the North Vietnamese. Indeed, every nation in the world that maintained diplomatic relations with Cambodia knew of the raids. Only the American people did not know.

When the North Vietnamese, Cambodian insurgents, and other communist nations accused the United States of aggression against a neutral nation, Americans could only consider this propaganda, when it actually had some basis in fact. Deceived on the bombing, Americans were again deceived about the accuracy of communist statements and the whole American role in the war. During the period of the bombing, there were a great many antiwar protests, along with some violence. The basis of the protests was that America's role was futile, illegal, and immoral. Even though the bombing of Cambodia was unknown in the United States, it nonetheless had a crucial effect on dissension over the war. Thus, the bombing had a great effect on American public opinion even though most Americans did not know the raids occurred.

Another nonevent. In 1975, Americans learned that the Central Intelligence Agency had engaged in widespread domestic spying activities, even though it is expressly forbidden by law from engaging in other than foreign intelligence gathering operations.

Following a newspaper exposé by Seymour Hersh of *The New York Times,* Vice-President Nelson Rockefeller was named to head a commission to investigate CIA operations. After months of study, the commission reported that the CIA had indeed burglarized and bugged homes of American citizens, tapped citizens' telephones, and opened their mail. It had unlawfully infiltrated antiwar groups and black radical organizations, accumulating files on 7,200 persons it considered dissidents. There were further charges that it sought to assassinate foreign leaders, even hiring known American criminals for this purpose. These types of activities went on for many years under several presidents and various CIA directors.

The general public may not have known of the CIA activities, but such actions could hardly be kept secret. A burglary rarely goes undiscovered. The victim knows and usually reports it to the police. Most people can tell if their mail has been opened. Information obtained from wiretapping and other bugging tactics usually circulates. Persons were known to have been fired from their jobs on the basis of CIA information. Meetings of dissident groups were disrupted. Generalized suspicion and disarray were caused among the groups infiltrated by the CIA. The criminal organization employed by the CIA certainly knew what the CIA was doing and took advantage of their governmental connection.* Public tranquility was hardly enhanced by any of these CIA activities. Rather, Americans experienced dissension and distrust, the causes of which were either mysterious or attributed to something else. People worried, for example, about a breakdown in morality or loss of respect for law and order when the real cause was the un-

---

* In a bizarre incident, a major criminal who had been hired to assassinate Premier Fidel Castro of Cuba got the CIA to do him a favor—bug a Las Vegas hotel room where he suspected his girl friend was meeting a prominent television entertainer. The nation's premier foreign intelligence organization was reduced to snooping into romantic entanglements for crooks.

known activities of the CIA. Again, our way of thinking about ourselves and our problems was greatly affected by events, even though we didn't know about them.

The CIA activities also illustrate an even greater threat to the way Americans think. Public opinion, which endorses the principle of government by law, is seriously affected by governmental lawlessness. The CIA operations were illegal on several scores. The 1947 act setting up the CIA expressly forbade it to engage in domestic spying. Aside from this, burglary, opening mail, and many types of wiretapping—let alone assassinating people—are illegal regardless of who does them and for what purpose.

The harm from such governmental lawlessness is both pervasive and potentially devastating. By definition, a democracy means that government exists by the consent of the governed—public opinion. A primary purpose of that government is to enact and enforce laws that benefit the nation, its people, and domestic order and stability. Without this, anarchy exists. When government itself becomes a criminal transgressor, the inevitable result is a massive breakdown in public acceptance of the law. In simplest language, the people (or many of them) say that if the government can break the law, why can't we? If government then uses its police powers to enforce the law on citizens, while breaking the law itself, the inevitable result is public distrust of government, as well as cynicism and apathy. Public attitudes are greatly altered. There is a breakdown of law and order. The nation becomes less democratic because the governmental actions are occurring without the consent of the governed. A fateful step toward totalitarianism has occurred.

The government, instead of serving the nation and the people, begins to serve itself. Secret criminal activity often has to be covered up by still more crimes. In a nation such as the United States, whose very essence is government by laws and not by men, governmental lawlessness, however noble its purpose, is merely lethal.

The revelations of deliberate deception and deceit in high levels of government has led to a national discussion of the problem of secrecy in government. Most people believe that some secrecy must occur. There are important national defense secrets to be protected, including weapons strength, deployment of forces, defense capabilities and plans. There are also diplomatic activities that should be secret. Public revelations would embarrass other nations, disrupt delicate diplomatic situations, and imperil peaceful relations.

There is also acceptance of the need for private discussions in government. Privacy permits officials to discuss problems frankly and freely, offering ideas and information and opinions they would hesitate to make in public. These discussions eventually lead to a policy decision and, it is hoped, an accurate public statement of what has been decided from the discussions. No one seriously suggests that every utterance of a president should be known to the public. He ought rather to be given an opportunity to formulate his thoughts and gather information before addressing the public.*

Yet, there is a general belief that governmental secrecy has been much abused. In the past, thousands of federal officials were empowered to classify, that is, make secret, government documents. Some absurdities occurred, such as classifying newspaper clippings and mail-order catalogs. In one exercise in futility, a memo was prepared and circulated urging that fewer documents be classified—and the memo was then classified. Abuse of secrecy made it extremely difficult for citizens to obtain information on governmen-

---

* A major exception was the Nixon administration. A secret recording system was installed to preserve every official word uttered in the White House. Mr. Nixon's aides declared this was intended for historical purposes. The tapes of conversations were to be edited for future use by scholars. The unedited tapes came to be used to discover that Mr. Nixon had lied about the Watergate affair. His resignation followed. Many people felt it was most unfortunate that the tapes were ever made and that the unexpurgated comments of Mr. Nixon and others were made public. Many who have heard the tapes report feeling embarrassed, as though they were eavesdropping on private affairs.

tal activities. Snooping, wiretapping, and other criminal activities were encouraged because the information obtained, as well as even the fact any information existed, could be kept secret.

In reaction to these abuses, Congress in 1975 amended the Freedom of Information Act to make it easier for citizens to obtain information on governmental activities, including access to files being maintained on them. Only certain types of information, such as defense secrets, were exempted from the act.

In the end, however, the untoward effects of secrecy, deception, and lies on public opinion can only be prevented by government officials themselves. On being sworn in as president in 1974, Gerald R. Ford promised an administration of openness and candor. It is possible that the American people will judge Mr. Ford and future presidents in terms of those qualities and that the memory of governmental deceit will fade.

CHAPTER FIVE   The News Media

On June 26, 1975, Prime Minister Indira Gandhi proclaimed a state of emergency in India. She suspended the basic freedoms in the world's most populous democracy, arrested her political opponents, and shuttered the offices of organizations she considered to be dissident.

Perhaps the most shocking element of India's slide into despotism was the rigid press censorship imposed by Mrs. Gandhi. In its August 4, 1975, issue, *Time* magazine described what it called a "stunning scene." More than 300 Indian and 75 foreign journalists were covering a session of the Indian Parliament. Every time an opposition member stood up to denounce Mrs. Gandhi and her actions, the journalists stopped writing and put away their notebooks. It was either that or go to jail. Mrs. Gandhi had imposed a Draconian gag rule, forbidding reporters from quoting opposition speakers, referring by name to any political prisoners, publishing anything "likely to denigrate the institutions of the Prime Minister or President" or even, indeed, to mention that censorship was occurring.

Mrs. Gandhi's action was simply a little more proof (if any were needed, so often has it occurred) that about the first action of any despotic or totalitarian government is to censor the press. Books, magazines, newspapers, and broadcasting stations are a prime source of information for the people. If that information can be controlled at its source, then public opinion can be controlled, that is, made favorable to the regime.

The founders of the United States—indeed, they were reacting to the insistence of the people—sought to prevent exactly this situation by guaranteeing a free press in this country. The First Amendment to the Constitution, the lead article in our cherished Bill of Rights, reads in its entirety:

> Congress shall make no law respecting an establishment of religion, or prohibiting the free exercise thereof; or abridging the freedom of speech, or of the press, or the right of the people peaceably to assemble, and to petition the government for a redress of grievances.

The First Amendment is the hallowed guarantee of liberty for the American people, and freedom of the press is listed third behind freedom of religion and freedom of speech as most precious to liberty. American journalists have vigorously defended press freedom throughout our history. Today, despite a few restrictions, such as laws against libel and slander, licensing of broadcasting stations, and recent attempts to compel reporters to reveal their sources of information, the United States has a level of press freedom perhaps unique in the world.

Many foreign leaders, notably the Russians and Chinese, have expressed amazement at the ability of the American news media to print and say just about anything. In its issue of August 4, 1975, *Time* quoted a Soviet diplomat as describing the relations between the American press and government as "anarchy." Ray Cline, a former deputy director of the CIA and now a director of the Georgetown University Center for Strategic and International Studies, was quoted by *Time* as joking: "The only unrestricted intelligence organization in this country is the American press."

Both the Soviet diplomat and the American were commenting on a story in the May 25, 1975, issue of *The New York Times*. The article revealed that American submarines, specially equipped with spying gear, had been monitoring Soviet missile activities for fifteen years, sometimes in USSR waters. The project had been code-named Holystone. As a result of the story, the Soviets stopped the submarine activities by planting mines in territorial waters and electronically jamming signals around missile sites. Because of the story, an important source of intelligence information was lost to the United States. Thus the consternation of Soviets and Americans that a newspaper story could have this effect.

This is but one of many thousands of possible examples of the running battle between the press and government that has marked our history. Rightly or wrongly, the American news media see themselves as virtually an unofficial branch of government with a duty to report government activity to the people, particularly activity they consider illegal, immoral, mistaken, or secret. And, most importantly, the news media believe they have a constitutional right to decide what to report and will not easily endure governmental interference in what they consider to be their prerogative. Throughout our history, officials at all levels of government have been annoyed and sometimes outraged at journalists. The general public usually has rather strong opinions on how well or poorly the news media are functioning.

There is no question that the news media have a potent effect upon the formation of public opinion in the United States. There is virtually no other way any person can obtain information about matters that he or she did not witness or experience than by reading about them, listening to them on the radio, or seeing them on television. Perhaps the only other way to obtain news is by word of mouth.

Most political scientists also agree that the news media play an unofficial but important function in the American system of government. One of the weaknesses in the system of government designed by the founders was an orderly process by which opponents of the government could express themselves. Most of the world's important democracies, such as Great Britain, Canada, France, the Scandinavian countries, Japan, and until recently India, have a parliamentary form of government in which the members of the minority party form what the British call the "loyal opposition." In parliamentary debate, the leader of the opposition is given ample opportunity to criticize the prime minister, who is expected to listen and reply. Even in India, Mrs. Gandhi, despite the arrests of opposition leaders, could not entirely silence her opponents in parliament. She could only silence the reporters covering it.

The United States has little that is similar. Congress has a great deal of debate on almost any matter. Opponents are given ample time to express themselves. But Congress has virtually no way to call a president before it, question him, and express opposition to his policies or actions. The president is elected separately from members of Congress. He is not a member of the legislative branch. He has his own constituency and under the Constitution is expected to maintain the principle of separation of powers between the executive, legislative, and judicial branches of government. He names members of his cabinet and other key federal agencies, most of whom serve as his pleasure. The person defeated in a presidential election has no role in government. He may not even be a member of government unless he coincidentally holds a Senate or House seat, as Senator McGovern did in 1972. Even then, he has no more power to oppose presidential policies than any other senator.

Clearly, the American system of government offers opponents of presidents very limited ability to question and criticize their policies. Enter the news media. They perform crucial roles in government by providing the opposition—be it to presidents, cabinet officials, Supreme Court justices, or members of Congress —a means to make their views known to the people. The news media also perform an equally crucial watchdog function. Reporters routinely question presidents about their actions and reasons for them. Reporters also report governmental actions and frequently ferret out information that government officials did not want known. A free press is considered a defense against governmental wrongdoing.

So important is a free press to the American scheme of government that if reporters were to be gagged, as was done in India, it would be a major alteration in our form of government. Doubt would exist, as in India, whether we were still a democracy.

A major issue of long-standing duration is how well or poorly the news media perform their important public-opinion and governmental functions. Critics of the media are legion, including most newsmen and newswomen themselves. The criticisms are frequently conflicting. The press is said both to report too much news and not enough, to be biased in its reporting and to not interpret the news enough, to be too sensational in its reporting of news events and to fail to pursue obvious evidences of wrongdoing, to be too critical of public officials and to be too friendly with them, to reflect centralized control of the news by giving too much power to a few people and to be too local and provincial in reporting the news.

The news media are said to be too conservative and too liberal, yet somehow be controlled by both monied interests and elitest thinking. A great many books and thousands of articles have been written both praising and denouncing the news media. We need to try to wend our way through this confusion.*

The most important fact to know about news media in America is its extremely fragmented nature. The most important news in this country is *local* news and it is served up by thousands of local

---

* In the analysis of the news media in this and the following chapter, I am relying most heavily on the usual sources—books and articles on the news media. Most are named in the text or in the reading list at the end of the book. To a lesser extent I am drawing on my own experiences. I cite these so the reader may evaluate them. I edited a frontline newspaper for a year during the Korean War in 1952–53; I worked as an announcer for two months late in 1953 at a small radio station in Marion, Ohio; for two weeks on the Marion, Ohio, *Star;* then two years (1954–56) on the Mansfield, Ohio, *News-Journal,* a paper of about 35,000 circulation and part of a small newspaper chain; then for eight years (1956–64) on the Baltimore *News American,* a large paper of more than 200,000 circulation owned by the Hearst Corporation. During this time and for some years after becoming a free-lance writer in 1964, I wrote several dozen articles for leading magazines. I have published about 40 books.

newspapers, local radio stations, and local television stations. Movies are shown in local theaters and books are sold in local stores or borrowed from local libraries. Decentralization and local autonomy are the hallmarks of the news media in the United States.

Unlike most countries, the United States has very little that qualifies as a national press, that is, newspapers widely read throughout the country. The most widely distributed newspaper in the United States is *The Wall Street Journal*, which is printed in six locations. It deals, however, largely with business and financial news. The same company publishes the *National Observer*, but it has a small circulation, as does the nationally distributed *Christian Science Monitor*.

The New York Times perhaps comes closest to being a national newspaper. It is widely read, frequently quoted, and has great influence, but even the million-plus circulation of its Sunday edition brings it into only a tiny percentage of American homes.

In his book *The Information Machines*, Ben H. Bagdikian points out that the metropolitan New York and Washington, D.C., newspapers together sell only 9.6 percent of the daily papers in the country. In contrast, the Moscow dailies have 87 percent of all circulation in the Soviet Union, the London papers 70 percent of the British circulation, and Tokyo papers 70 percent of the Japanese readership. This pattern is repeated in most of the nations of the world. A few large papers reach most of the readers, giving the entire population the same news and point of view.

In contrast, Americans receive their printed news from more than 1,700 daily newspapers. These vary in an almost infinite number of ways in terms of size, ownership, editorial opinion, and the completeness and competence with which they report the news. A few maintain reporters in Washington and a relative handful station correspondents overseas. Most of the dailies receive their national and international news by teletype either from the Associated Press or United Press International, our two national news wire services. AP and UPI maintain a staff of reporters worldwide to gather and disseminate the news. A single reporter may be covering a large area, such as the Middle East or India.

It might be said that AP and UPI act as a national press. In those 1,700 daily newspaper offices, clacking teletype machines (and other devices) provide basically the same news story throughout the nation. But, any of several things happen to that story when it reaches the editorial offices of the newspaper. It may not be used at all. Indeed, that is most likely to be the result. Newspapers receive far, far more news than they can possibly print. Most of the wire service news is simply thrown away. If the story is printed, it may be cut to only a few paragraphs. It may be put inside on some little-read page. It may be reduced to a single column and graced with a small headline so that it receives little notice from hurried readers.

The editors of every daily newspaper, including most of those owned by large newspaper chains, have the prerogative to decide what news goes in the paper. Indeed, it is the major decision they make each day—and it is an exceedingly complex one. Some factors: The paper is of a certain size. The editors know how many pages are to be printed, a decision dictated by the size of the presses, the number of pages of advertising, and even the availability of newsprint or paper.

The number of pages or columns available to the editors is further reduced by regular features, which readers are accustomed to seeing. Examples are the funnies, puzzles and games, syndicated columns, the editorial page. No editor would dream of throwing out "Peanuts" or "Blondie" to make room for a news story. His telephone would never stop ringing with protests.

Of the remaining columns for news stories, a high percentage will go for purely local news stories written by local reporters. The editor knows that his readers are interested in local news— crime, fires, accidents, local sports teams, politics, school ac-

tivities, the town budget, weddings and social events, and the activities of local clubs and organizations. People like to read about
their friends in the newspaper and, even better, see their own name
and if possible their photograph. At times local news will drive
nearly all national and international news out of the paper. As
one of my editors once put it, "A local fistfight is more news
than a riot in India." Even if a person reads the newspaper
thoroughly—and surveys show that few people do—that person
will receive only a tiny fraction of the national and international
news.

The effect of the space limitations and the judgmental decisions
of editors on what news to print is to reduce greatly the role of
AP and UPI as a national press. Perhaps only a handful (sometimes
only one or two, maybe none) of the top national and international
stories as run by AP and UPI are printed in all 1,700 daily
newspapers. Even then, the story will be "played" differently in
each paper. Some papers will give it greater prominence than others, use larger type for the headlines, and so forth. Also the word-
ing of the headline will vary in each paper, giving the hurried
reader who only glances at the headlines an impression of the news
of the day that may differ greatly from the impression of another
person reading a different newspaper.

It is not possible to overemphasize the importance of the fact
that the United States, unlike most countries, has no national press
presenting uniform information and viewpoints to a majority of
citizens. Americans receive a variety of information, depending
on where they live and what paper they read. It is difficult for
even the president or other national leaders to reach Americans
with the same news story. Thus it is hard to form a consensus
in the United States because the information we receive from
newspapers comes in so many different forms and is so subject
to manipulation by omission, prominence, headline, and other devices.

Something similar happens in radio news broadcasting. Of the thousands of radio stations in the United States virtually all are locally owned and operated. The decision on the amount of air time given to news is the prerogative of the station management. A handful of "all news" radio stations offer nothing but news and news features all day long. Most stations offer a great deal of music—and commercials—and schedule five-minute newscasts every hour or half hour, with longer periods of news at regular intervals.

There are exceptions, notably the all-news stations, but most radio news has two major characteristics. It is very brief and highly repetitious. Most news on radio is reduced to a few sentences about the story and frequently is little more than a headline. Radio newscasters will prepare and read a summary of the day's top events. This will be repeated with little change every half hour or hour, unless some new major event or story dictates a change. As in newspapers, a sizable percentage of the radio news will be local news.

Television news is something else. The broadcasting stations are usually locally owned and operated, but these stations are extremely dependent for their shows on either syndicated programs, which they can purchase, or shows provided by the television networks to which they subscribe—the American Broadcasting Company (ABC), Columbia Broadcasting System (CBS), or the National Broadcasting Company (NBC).

Most television stations maintain a local news staff, airing local news programs, generally in the morning, evening, and late at night. The quality of local news coverage varies, but every station tries to film or videotape important local news events. Other brief news stories are read by a newscaster or reporter. Some of these local news programs are excellent in terms of the diversity of news and news features they carry. Station WNBC, Channel 4, in New York City, for example, carries two hours of mostly local news from 5:00 to 7:00 every weekday evening. All stations carry a half hour or hour of local news every evening.

Television does something that no print or other broadcast medium does. Each network offers an hour or more a day of national and international news, undiluted by local news, and beamed into many millions of homes. Each network offers a half hour of national news every evening. Each network also has lengthy morning programs devoted to news and news features.

Network television news has great impact. Most Americans now receive more information about national and international events from television than any other source. In addition, the three networks, as well as the Public Broadcasting System (PBS) devote generous time to coverage of special events, such as presidential speeches, elections, space shots, and important news stories, as well as analysis of major news events and national issues.

Despite the time given to network news on television, its major characteristic is *extreme brevity*. A great deal of important news is omitted entirely. Major stories that might command a column or two in major daily newspapers will be reduced to a few seconds, seldom more than a minute or two on the network news. There are many other criticisms of TV news (to be considered shortly), yet the fact remains that most Americans receive their national news from the tube.

The impact of television on public opinion is immense. There are a number of reasons for this to be considered in chapter 7, but at this point we can cite the fact that network television news is our *only* source of uniform national news. The evening news programs, as well as news feature and special event programs, are beamed identically into every home where people watch that particular network. Where there are 1,700 different ways of reporting the news in the newspapers, there are precisely three—ABC, CBS, and NBC—of reporting network television news. And, few people are able to watch more than one network at a time. The White House has a set showing three channels at once, but how the president can listen to three stations at the same time is difficult to understand.

The simple fact that network television is our only source of uniform national news makes it of the utmost importance in providing the information—or lack of it—that so greatly influences why we think as we do. The television networks therefore have a unique opportunity for molding public opinion in the United States.

The other major source of news for Americans is the news weeklies, principally *Newsweek, Time* and *U.S. News and World Report*. These offer summaries of the week's major news. The stories usually offer a great deal of analysis and interpretation.

In sum, Americans receive a great deal of local news and relatively small amounts of national and international news. Many persons have sought to analyze why the United States has no national press to shape public opinion. Among the reasons given is the size of the country, although that has not bothered the Russians who have a centralized press. The First Amendment is often cited as a reason for the plethora of local newspapers. Anyone can start a paper. No laws can impinge on that paper's freedom to publish just about anything it wants.

A more important reason is the federal system of government. The United States consists of one national government based in Washington, 50 state governments, and more than 91,000 local governments and taxing authorities. Despite all the attention paid to events in Washington, most government in this country is state and local government. Such diverse matters as schools, street paving, snow removal, parking, zoning and housing codes, garbage collection, mass transit, libraries, police and fire protection, public welfare, and dozens of other services are activities of local government, even if some of the funding comes from the federal government.

These are the daily concerns of citizens. They want to read and hear about these matters. There is no way a paper in New York or

Washington or a station in Chicago or Los Angeles can report the school events of Tuscaloosa, Alabama, Waterloo, Iowa, or Walla Walla, Washington. A diversity of local news media is inevitable in the United States. It is also inevitable that the news dispensed will vary greatly, leaving the impact on public opinion to vary greatly.

Yet, despite the number and diversity of local news outlets, the point is consistently made that the United States needs a greater variety of news outlets. Only a few cities in the United States have genuinely competing newspapers and generally not more than two. New York, which once had more than a score of newspapers, now has only three. Many quite large cities do not have any competing newspapers. The city may have two newspapers, morning and evening, but both papers are owned by the same publishing company. Very frequently, the newspaper will also own a television and radio station.

The criticism is made that ownership of news media is too closely held, that citizens of quite large communities are too dependent upon the whims and attitudes of a single publisher, that there is not enough variety of editorial opinions being offered to the public.

There is some truth to this. A century ago, Americans read much different types of papers. In the presidential election of 1876, *The New York Times*—today a staid paper trying to be unbiased— openly supported Rutherford B. Hayes. Its news columns were filled with the most scurrilous attacks on his opponent, Democrat Samuel J. Tilden. Fortunately, New Yorkers could also buy the *Herald*, which adored Tilden and scurrilously attacked Hayes. Today, if a particular newspaper supports or condemns a candidate or issue, it is not very easy to find another newspaper with a different or opposing viewpoint except in those cities (less than a dozen), including New York, which still have competing, separately owned newspapers.

Most newspaper publishers and editors try to relieve the dangers of centralized ownership by simply being fair. An effort is made to be objective in reporting, although critics suggest that objectivity frequently means being only bland and confusing. A variety of viewpoints is solicited, if only in man-on-the-street interviews. Editorial pages usually carry a variety of columns offering conservative, liberal, and moderate views on public issues. We will consider how well these devices work in the next chapter.

CHAPTER SIX

The Power of the Press— and Why

An axiomatic statement in the Army is that the most important rank is private, the lowest rank. A general may be a brilliant tactician, but he will be replaced if he cannot command the discipline and loyalty of common soldiers who do the fighting and dying.

Something similar happens in every business, including the news media business. The most important person on the newspaper is the reporter. The publisher and editor may be excellent at their tasks, but in the end they must rely on the efforts of reporters, who perform the basic job. In the news business, the final product is shaped more from the bottom up, from reporters to editors, than it is from the top down, editors to reporters.

The reporter's power is increasing. Years ago, when there were many competing newspapers, the accuracy of a reporter's work could be checked against his rivals on competing newspapers. Many a reporter was hauled on the carpet a generation ago for neglecting to learn some information a rival paper had. Or, if he had a scoop or beat on his rivals, he was asked to verify his information. Today's reporter seldom sees a rival from another paper, at least in covering local news. His work is not easily checked. He is on his own. His accuracy is less often questioned.

By definition, the act of reporting an event, whether it be a presidential news conference or an automobile accident on Main Street, is the act of compiling the facts about the happening. He or she will use a variety of methods to accomplish this. The reporter will rely on official documents, such as court records, reports of police or fire officers, official minutes of meetings, prepared speeches, printed press releases (called "handouts" in newspaper parlance), and similar devices. The reporter who is present at an event takes notes, asks questions, makes observations, interviews participants or witnesses. The reporter has a moral, legal, and professional obligation to perform these tasks as accurately as humanly possible.

Most reporters do their work well, perhaps even extraordinarily well considering the often difficult circumstances under which it is performed. In the end, however, the reporter is just about the sole judge of the facts. He cannot learn all the facts, nor does he want to know everything. He wants to report the most important or pertinent facts and do so in a descending order of importance. In an automobile accident, for example, the most important fact is whether anyone is killed. The second most important fact is whether anyone was injured. Thus the "lead" on the accident story might read: "Two were killed and three injured in a five-car pileup on Route 80 today."

This is a rather simple, clear-cut example. The problem becomes more involved if the reporter covers the mayor's speech on traffic safety. The reporter must make a judgment of what was most important in the mayor's remarks. Was it his statement that he was asking police to crack down on speeders? Or that he was appointing a blue-ribbon traffic safety commission? Or his denouncement of Detroit auto makers for building high-speed cars?

In making his judgment on the most important facts from the speech, the reporter may consult with his editors, so that a collective opinion is reached. But if the reporter misses the fact that the mayor was ordering the speed limit reduced to twenty-five miles an hour throughout the city, or did not think it important enough to report, then there really isn't very much to be done about it—except for the editors to criticize the reporter's work, if the omitted fact ever becomes known.

When the reporter writes and files the story, the editor makes a decision on its importance. It may call for a banner headline or be buried inside or anywhere in between. A headline of a certain size and typeface will be ordered for the story. In all but the smaller papers, the headline will be written by a copy editor. His or her task will be the difficult one of choosing a few words that describe the story. If the headline is very large, the copy editor may have only two or three words to describe the story. He seldom gets more than six or eight words. Thus the headline may come out: MAYOR CRACKS DOWN ON SPEEDERS or SPEEDERS BEWARE—MAYOR or MAYOR NAMES PANEL TO PROBE ACCIDENTS.

This brief glimpse of some of the nuts and bolts of journalism is apropos to a major charge leveled against the news media—that they engage in bias, distorting the news. In his book, *Don't Blame the People*, Robert Cirino offers a "catalog of hidden bias," listing thirteen common biases of news media. These include the source, selection and omission of news, the placement of stories, the words, headlines, photographs and captions of photographs. He also lists a number of "myths" of news media, including the myths of objectivity and fairness. Most libraries contain several books detailing similar abuses.

It is possible to publish a photograph of the president that shows him in a dignified, thoughtful demeanor or perhaps smiling and shaking hands with well-wishers. It is also possible to publish photographs of the president frowning, yawning, yelling, scratching, eating, drinking, or performing a number of other humorous or undignified actions. The choice of photograph is positively guaranteed to both please and displease some readers and cause a charge of bias to be made or thought. Those who like the president and his policies will be pleased by the dignified photograph and displeased by the one showing him in an unfavorable light. Those who dislike the president and his policies will have opposite reactions.

The important question is whether that photograph, and all the other evidences of bias in news articles, headlines, and placement, is deliberate bias. There are those who see an elaborate conspiracy in the choice of photographs. They envision the publisher or editor coming out of his office and saying, "Use that photo of the president. It makes him look like a fool." Something similar to this does happen, but probably only rarely.

Far more likely the photograph was used because it was (a) the latest available of the president; (b) it fit the space available for a photograph; or (c) it appealed to editors as an unusual one or one of photographic merit. The decision on which photograph to use was probably made casually and in a great hurry. Little or no thought was given to whether it was a favorable or unfavorable photo of the president and to what its possible effects on readers might be. Something similar happens with headlines, words, placement, and other evidence of "hidden bias." Such bias is inevitable. Most newspapermen and women know they cannot please everyone. They don't really try to please anyone other than themselves.

The more serious bias of the news media occurs in other ways. However rarely, it does happen that publishers and editors order "campaigns." A managing editor may declare a traffic safety campaign. As a result, there will be more diligent reporting of traffic accidents, which will receive greater prominence in the newspaper. Particular traffic hazards will be reported. A reporter may be assigned to write an article or series of articles on traffic safety, traffic hazards, and the city's efforts to cope with the problem. Interviews will be made with safety experts. The plight of victims will be reported in sob stories. Such activities are routine in the news media. A former city editor of mine would summarily declare a "crime wave" to enliven a dull news day. It consisted of nothing more than in-depth reporting of fairly routine crimes for a few days, using larger type in the headlines.

Contrary to the popular image, newspaper offices are mostly dull places. Newspaper people like excitement, big, important stories, a great rush to meet deadlines, crises that keep the adrenalin flowing. If such events do not occur naturally, they have a tendency to create them by enlarging events so as to make the news exciting and interesting. No reporter ever went out to cover a dull story. If at all possible, he will make it interesting and important, trying as hard as possible to get it on page one with a by-line. It is human nature.

Newsmen and women are also artists, and that is important. More esoteric critics may not rank journalism among the fine arts of literature and drama, but the simple fact is that print and broadcast journalism involves the act of creativity. Newspaper reporters are judged not solely on their ability to gather facts, but on how well they write them into a story. For generations, many of America's leading writers learned their craft in journalism. Radio and television reporters are judged not only for their information, but for the dramatic quality of their delivery. There is a bit of actor or actress in every television newscaster. Every journalist therefore feels a powerful thrust toward literary and dramatic excellence. His personal success in his career will be measured by his artistry as well as his reporting. Art and facts do not always mix. There are times when every journalist will sacrifice facts for art. Bias thereby occurs.

Most reporters also have ego problems. To a person, they are fairly ordinary individuals in terms of intelligence, education, and talent. Most are not particularly well paid. Their incentives are glory and power. Reporters on large papers tend to cover presidents, governors, mayors, celebrities, and important events. It is heady stuff to have prominent people acknowledge your presence, greet you by name, recognize your importance, even ask your opinion.

At any event, the reporter's presence is observed. A special place is set aside for him. A special effort is made to give him special access to information. If this does not occur, if prominent people in some way annoy the reporter or incur his wrath, he is in a position to harm them in extremely subtle ways—by omission, by giving less importance to them, by choice of words that color the meaning of the events.* Even the lowliest reporter can have extraordinary power in a specific situation. He knows it. He relishes it. He uses it.

Behind the reporter is a series of editors who have, enjoy, and use great power over the reporter's story, its editing, and its placement, The editors—except the top editors—may be desk-bound and no longer hobnobbing with prominent people, but they have a lot to say about the coverage those prominent people get. The editors often use their power like a sword and for personal reasons.

Those who see a political conspiracy in the news media might better see a case of personal aggrandizement. It is said that all men are motivated by money, power, or glory. Among print and broadcast journalists, the primary motives—all exceptions duly noted— are first power and second glory. The reporters and editors relish their power to determine what shall be reported and how extensively. They also wish to advance their own careers. The by-line— one's name on a story or a few seconds on national television news—is tremendously heady stuff, proof of professional excellence. Just watch the next televised presidential news conference. Chances are that those clamoring hands and calls of "Mr. President" reflect not so much a desire to ask an important question as a desire to be recognized by the president and to appear on national television. Both are proof that one is important in one's job.

Journalists suffer from self-importance. The act of being a journalist makes them some kind of celebrity. If Walter Cronkite and John Chancellor, to give two examples, were in the exterminating business, they would not be invited to posh Washington parties and White House banquets.

---

* To give one example, most public persons being quoted expect the reporter to "clean up" their language, omitting mistakes in grammar, poor sentence structure, and so forth. Only rarely is an exact quote precisely what the person said. If a reporter wishes to make a person "look bad," it is a simple matter to quote the person exactly, bad grammar, fuzzy thinking and all.

Reporters realize their tremendous power. By being at the scene of a news event, they are in the position—sometimes they are the only persons so situated—to determine what information the public will receive about what has happened. They know full well that the facts they select to report and the words they choose in writing or describing the news event will determine in large measure what the public thinks about the event. Their influence on public opinion is little short of stupendous. Thus, because they so influence what the public thinks, reporters are in the position of making as well as reporting news.

Journalists make news in another way. Every public official from the president on down is influenced in his actions—and in a major way—by what he believes the press will report. The official tries to take actions that will be reported favorably by the press. If he believes the press reports will be unfavorable, he will often attempt to manipulate—the most used word is "manage"—the news reports through various types of concealment of facts, deception, half-truths, altered emphasis, silence (the famous "no comment" answer to a question), and just plain obfuscation so as to utter something while actually saying nothing of substance. Because the reporter forces the public official to alter his actions and utterances with an eye to news reports, the reporters thereby make news.

This meshing of journalism and government occurs in every city hall, state house, and bureaucratic office in the land, and all of it has a powerful impact on what Americans know and thereby think. Its best evidence is at the national scene. Every recent president has hired a press secretary. Ron Nessen, a former television newsman, fulfilled this function for President Ford. Mr. Nessen's (and his predecessors' in other administrations) most ostensible function was to represent the President to the press. He appeared before them, made announcements of news, answered questions, etc. Mr. Nessen also had a reverse function. He represented the press to Mr. Ford. Mr. Nessen was in daily contact with the President advising him on what the press was asking, what the press's reaction to a certain event was likely to be, how a statement might be phrased so as to achieve a desirable impression in news reports, when the best timing of a presidential action or announcement might be, and much more. Before a presidential news conference, Mr. Nessen and his staff briefed the President on the questions likely to be asked by reporters and recommended suitable answers for him.

The role of presidential press secretary is a singularly difficult one. He stands between the president, who wishes to maintain his freedom of action, and a large press corps that sees its duty as learning everything and reporting it. Mr. Nessen had maintained amicable relations with the press, largely because he had sought to be as open and truthful as possible.

The most difficult role of press secretary in memory was the unenviable position of Ron Ziegler for President Nixon. Mr. Nixon disliked and distrusted the press. He tended to use Mr. Ziegler not so much as a conduit of information, but as a door blocking the path of information from the White House to pressroom. Reporters criticized Mr. Ziegler (sometimes caustically) for engaging in obfuscation, misrepresentation, deception, and out-and-out lies with the intent to conceal information. That Mr. Ziegler uttered lies has been proven many times. What has not been established is whether he told falsehoods personally or whether he simply did not know the truth.

The Nixon administration provided hosts of examples of the power of the press to make news by influencing government actions. Consider just one, the secret bombing of Cambodia. As we have seen, it went on for years and was known throughout the world, but not by the American people. Why were the raids kept secret? President Nixon and his military advisors obviously felt the raids were necessary in fighting the war in Vietnam, which lies adjacent to Cambodia. That military necessity could have been explained to the American people. It might be suggested that the raids were kept secret for diplomatic reasons; we did not wish to admit we were bombing a neutral nation. Perhaps, but the Cambodian government and people certainly knew we were bombing them. Secrecy was pointless in this regard. The most logical reason for the secrecy was fear that the press in America would report the raids in such a way as to stir up further opposition to American involvement in the war. The action of keeping the raids secret, and engaging in great deception to do so, was probably dictated as much by fear of the press as by any other reason. Thus, the press influenced government. It made news. And public opinion was greatly affected.

Journalists know the power that derives from selecting the facts and writing and describing them. Virtually all reporters try hard to be responsible about this power. Indeed, it is the hardest part of their jobs. Reporters use a number of techniques to try to reduce the amount of personal bias and ax grinding that creeps into their news accounts, although they realize even these will not guarantee one hundred percent effectiveness all the time.

Some of these techniques are worth examining, for they can arm the newspaper reader or radio and television listener with the ability to judge how unbiased a report is. One technique is for the reporter to recognize honestly his own opinions and attitudes. He or she then bends over backwards to report as fairly and as abundantly as possible that information with which he disagrees. There is a risk of going too far, however. In an important gubernatorial election some years ago, one of the candidates complained that a reporter covering his campaign for a major paper was biased against him and asked the paper to withdraw him and substitute another reporter. This was done. The simple facts were that the reporter was a member of the candidate's political party, admired and respected him, and indeed voted for him.

Another technique, widely used, is to keep all color words out of news accounts and so restrict the use of adjectives and other descriptive words and phrases so as to make the report extremely dull and boring. But this technique also omits many of the ways in which bias and slant gets into a news account.

Still another technique, also widely used, is for the reporter to rigidly restrict the news accounts to the immediate facts of the event. He avoids giving background information or making comparisons with similar events in the past simply because by so doing the reporter may cause the reader to have a particular interpretation of the meaning and importance of what has happened. This is why so many news stories seem to stand alone with little relation to other events. This technique may reduce the amount of slant in a story, but it adds to public confusion about the meaning of a news event. Newspapers try to offset such confusion by printing interpretive stories, frequently labeled as news analyses or news features, and by printing editorials and signed columns discussing the event. Weekly and monthly news magazines, because they are not under the daily pressure of newspaper publication, generally offer a great deal more background and interpretation of events. They are thereby much more biased.

Perhaps the reporter's best defense against his own bias is his ferocious dedication to the news and the reporting of it. The biggest pitfall of a journalist is that he may become so committed to a person, a cause, a friendly news source, that he loses his objectivity and begins to represent the person or cause and not his newspaper or broadcast facility. When this happens, he is finished as a reporter, although he may continue to be employed as one, and has become a public relations man.

Reporters take a number of actions to guard against this pitfall. Many become militant nonjoiners of organizations, refusing membership in anything to maintain their independence of reporting. The reporter learns to question everything and everybody, to search for more facts, to ask the impertinent question, to doubt motives of just about everyone. He may develop a facade of cynicism about people and causes. If he covers a regular beat, he will come to feel it is his duty to learn everything, particularly if someone does not want him to know it. He will snoop, pry, even bribe. In fact, he will do just about anything to gain access to news that he feels is important. He is compulsive in his belief that he has a *right* to know. And, in covering his beat, he will assert his independence of the news sources by reporting what they do not want the public to know, especially including the fact they did not *want* the public to know. The risk is that the reporter may grossly interfere with the actions of public officials and force them into greater and greater efforts at secrecy, which happened with the Nixon administration. The reporter replies that all secrecy is bad and that it is better if he and the public know everything.*

To sum up, most of the real power to manipulate and distort news information lies with the individual reporter. He tries to guard against it. His editors, experienced in these matters, look for evidence of bias and remove it, or warn him. As a protection against reportorial bias, editors frequently transfer reporters to a different beat so they do not become too involved with particular news courses. Many reporters, particularly those assigned to Washington as correspondents and are called home for new assignments, dislike having their beats changed.

Yet, there is no way a human being can eliminate all of his bias. It is only amazing that American journalists remain as unbiased as they are.

This great emphasis on the reporter's role in influencing why we think as we do has been made here to try to counteract the widespread public notion that journalistic bias is somehow dictated by publishers and top editors. Some people feel that publishers and

---

* Though beyond the subject of this book, a serious debate in journalism is whether the press should ever keep anything secret. Many argue that the press should remain silent about certain defense and diplomatic secrets, the revelation of which might harm the nation. Others argue that by withholding information, the press is becoming a tool of government and part of government, sacrificing its independence and surrendering its watchdog role over government activities. The dangers of secrecy are far greater, in this view, than the inconvenience publishing information causes the government. Newspapers should be in the business of publishing news, not in the business of protecting government secrets.

owners of broadcast facilities engage in some form of conspiracy to control elections, influence government, and manipulate public opinion on behalf of their pet ideas.

It does happen. There are a good many publications and broadcast stations that bray their political, economic, and social ideas, usually of an extremist nature. But these views and the trumpeting of them are usually so blatant as to be obvious to the reader or listener. About the only people convinced are those who already agree with the views. Such journalistic enterprises are simply far less of a threat to manipulation of public opinion than that subtle bias disguised as objective reporting.

Every newspaper has policies it espouses. Most publishers and editors feel duty bound to take a stand on public issues. The paper's policies are mainly restricted to the editorial page. In the case of broadcasting stations, open opinion is presented in short editorials. The overwhelming majority of public matters do not command an editorial position, at least in the early stages.

If there is a policy, publishers and editors will generally not try to inflict it on the reporter. The ethics of the profession command that the reporter be given the independence to report the facts as he or she learns them. It is anathema to editorial employees to have advertising, circulation, or other business departments even suggest what news ought to appear in the newspaper. At the same time, the editors know that unless the paper makes money, they will all lose their jobs. So, a kind of grudging accommodation takes place. A certain number of public relations and puff pieces appear to please advertisers. Editors and reporters will at least try not to offend important advertisers. If the paper is weak financially, a bit more effort may be made.

On matters of public policy, members of the newsroom will pay scant attention to the activities of editorial writers. The front office will not try to dictate the coverage of a particular story. At the same time the reporters and editors know they are not long for their jobs, or at least on that assignment, if they depart too much from the stated policies of the paper. If the reporter undermines the newspaper policy, he will be quite subtle about it. Probably every publisher and editor feels victimized by his reporters at least once in a while for reporting news unfavorable to the paper's policy, and every reporter feels that his freedom to write what he truly knows is impinged by his superiors. Either the story wasn't used or was cut in some way to embrace a newspaper's policy.

These instances, however, are far less common than most people think. Most papers today, perhaps because of the lack of competing papers in the same town, take pride in the conflict of ideas and viewpoints that grace their pages. Journalistic ax grinding is far less prevalent than it was even a few years ago—and shrinking.

Still, it is a good idea for a person to read a variety of newspapers and publications that offer differing information and viewpoints on public affairs. He will be making his own defense against biased manipulation of the way he thinks. Unfortunately, this is extremely difficult in the case of television news, a problem we consider next.

CHAPTER SEVEN

How Television Distorts the
News—and Why

The problems of selecting and slanting the news, which are
enacted daily in thousands of newspaper offices and radio stations
across the land, are tremendously magnified on network television simply because this is our only source of uniform national
news. The decision on what to report at 7:00 each evening and how
is a most difficult one. And because of the exclusive nature of network news, its editors and reporters receive a barrage of criticism
from those who know its importance and impact and thereby dislike its effects.

Network television news is in the unenviable position of never
being able to please everyone. Newspapers and magazines have this
problem, too. But the problem is worse for broadcasters because
they are subject to government regulation by the Federal Communications Commission. Stations can lose their license for untoward
actions, including extreme bias in news reporting. A television reporter simply has to be far more careful and circumspect than a
newspaper reporter. Television executives and reporters decry federal regulation as an intolerable burden on freedom of the press.

It is not possible to exaggerate the impact of television news.
Sitting in our homes, we see and hear events half a world away.
Those same sights and sounds are uniform in every home in the
nation. Their impact on the formation of public opinion could not
possibly be greater. If we try to set aside the issues of whether television news is good or bad, properly or improperly done, we can
perhaps arrive at some understanding of the problems of network
news presentation so as to realize how we are being influenced by it.

Television news is made possible, and cursed, by the movie

camera and the microphone. Sight and sound are both recorded, meshed on to sound film and videotape, and shown on the television news. Again, that which makes the news possible in every home also greatly alters the news in most significant ways. Every person should be aware of how this occurs.

The camera is not a human eye, and a microphone is not a person's ears. Neither device comes equipped with the human brain. A human being can enter a crowded room in which a great many people are talking all at once. At first the person hears only a great hubbub of talk. Then, shortly, his attention is drawn to the talk of a single person or group of people. The human ear—brain, really—can tune out all other noise and concentrate on a single voice or conversation. A television sound technician can also do this. By placement of the microphones, he can pick up the general room noise, then zero in on a particular voice or conversation.

But the human brain can do something that the microphone can do only with the greatest difficulty, if at all. The brain can hear simultaneous conversations. It has the capacity to flit instantly back and forth between two, three, or more conversations, picking out a word or phrase here and there to gather most of the meanings of all conversations. The eye-brain does something similar, seeing the total and all the individual parts, making an impression that is both a compilation of parts and a whole. This is impossible for a camera, even in the most artistic hands.

The human brain is far more capable than the camera or microphone. Consider a football game. The camera may show the players huddling, then lining up, the quarterback barking signals, then going back to pass. The trajectory of the ball is shown, the player catching it and being tackled. The noise of the crowd is heard, the sound of whistles. But the people in the stands saw much more: the sun and sky, the people in the stands, the players on the bench, the coaches pacing the sidelines, the whole field of play, the flanker who ran down the field as a decoy, the player who blocked, the pile up of players, the quarterback who was knocked down after the pass was thrown—much, much more that the camera cannot record. The spectator heard individual sounds from the stands, even the field.

Many studies have been published showing the difference in impressions received between spectators at an event and television viewers. A common experience is that the home viewer is able to see and hear better. Particularly if there is a large crowd, the spectator may be a long distance away. His view may be obstructed. Listening to a speech or music may be difficult because of the crowd noises. The spectator may therefore know less of what is transpiring, be confused and distracted. In contrast, the television camera can zoom in for close-ups of specific people or actions. Microphones can be placed so that sounds are clearly heard in living rooms. An announcer will explain exactly what is going on.

The ability to render clear, close-up photos and sound is the great virtue of television. But the act of doing this involves a process of selection of what is to be shown and heard. This selection is made by camera and sound experts and by directors—people. Instantly, a human judgment is made of what is to be seen and heard. The same sort of editorial opinion and opportunity for bias as occurs in newspapers enters into television. And the bias has more impact, because the selected sights and sounds are being transmitted into the viewer's home. The viewer believes he has witnessed and heard an event, a battle, a speech, whatever. It is hard for the viewer to realize that he or she is seeing only *part* of what transpired and that some individual made a choice of what was seen. If another part was shown, a much different impression might have been given.

The camera and microphone also pose a tremendous logistics problem. Under the best of circumstances, the camera and microphone are bulky to carry around. Several people are involved in making the sound film or tape. The equipment is extremely expensive. There is no way for television crews to be everywhere that news is occurring. Indeed, television can report only the tiniest fraction of the day's events.

Television networks make great efforts to photograph as much of the news as possible. Camera crews are sent to the scene of fires, floods, and other natural disasters and accidents. The crews try to get there while the event is occurring. More frequently, they arrive after the event and film its results. Police officers and witnesses will be interviewed. All of this is similar to the techniques used by a newspaper reporter. It might have the advantage of allowing television viewers to be in the role of reporters, seeing and hearing for themselves, except that the film or tape is edited by someone who makes a judgment of what will appear on the tube.

Because of the bulkiness of television equipment, TV newsmen, more than print reporters, need to anticipate the news. By knowing when an event is likely to occur in the future, the camera and sound crews can be sent ahead. Their equipment can be put in place, the lighting set up, and the sound and camera angles tested. Even better, facilities can be created on a rather permanent basis at places where news frequently occurs, such as the White House, Capitol, United Nations, and other such places. The president or a member of Congress can come to a particular place for his appearance on television.

The effect is to distort the news by emphasizing events that occur at certain, prearranged locations. It is inevitable that a high percentage of the television news emanates from Washington, specifically from the White House and Capitol. Appearances by the president or prominent members of Congress are routine. Far less coverage is given to the actions of cabinet members, important officials of the bureaucracy, military officers, governors, mayors, businessmen, and educators—simply because it is difficult for the television crews to be present in all the places a news story is developing. In contrast, a newspaper person carries only a pencil and notebook. He can telephone people. Television must have more—sound film.

Television news is in the movie business. The very nature of the medium means that there must be motion pictures to portray or illustrate the news. A TV newscast cannot consist of a reporter or anchorman, no matter how handsome and articulate, sitting before the camera reading the news. There must be film or tape of people doing something—*action*. As anyone who has ever taken home movies knows, the product isn't very good if the movie shows only grandma, Aunt Helen, or the kids standing there posing as for a still shot. In home movies, the aim is to catch people unaware, candidly, moving about in some form of action. Professional TV cameramen have the same aim, to catch on film action that is interesting, dramatic, exciting.

Wittingly or unwittingly, the content of network television news is dictated by the availability of action film or tape. If there is an important story for which no film is available, the anchorman will simply read the news or switch over to a filmed segment of a reporter standing in front of the White House or Capitol or some such place to read a brief account of the news event. This, of course, is not action film, but it gives the impression of action by showing a reporter at the scene and on the job. There are a variety of techniques to mask the lack of action film. A still picture may be run. Old film may be resurrected from the files and shown as background for the news story or as an example of a similar event. In covering court trials, where cameras are prohibited, television regularly shows an artist's sketch of a courtroom scene while the announcer reads a few sentences about the trial.

Such techniques are poor substitutes for action film. No newscaster, news editor, or program director would want a whole half hour of news composed of such makeshift appearances of action. They want action film. And when they have some, there is an irresistible temptation to bend—distort—the news of the day so that a good piece of film can be used. The riot in India, the civil war in Lebanon, the famine in Africa, the slaughtering of calves in Minnesota as a protest against low farm prices, the political campaign in Alabama, may not have been the most important news of the day. These stories may not have appeared in any of the 1,700 daily newspapers. But they are shown on network news because good action film was available in the studio. To make an event more important on the evening news than it really is just because film happens to be available is a tremendous distortion of the news.

Even if the event is important and worthy of several minutes on the evening news, the need for action film creates other types of distortion. The anchorman may report that a ceasefire agreement has been reached in Lebanon (or elsewhere) and then show film of violence taken a day or days before, which just reached the studios. A short piece of film of Dr. Henry Kissinger, the American Secretary of State, landing in Cairo on a Middle East peace mission may be juxtapositioned with a newly acquired piece of film showing a firebrand extremist vowing to continue fighting until his demands are met. A statement by a Washington official urging Americans to save on fuel consumption may be accompanied by a film featuring the opening of oil wells in the North Sea. The result of all such devices is confusion, altered impact, distortion of the events of the day.

The need for action film leads to a far more serious distortion of the news. There isn't much action in sitting, reading, writing, or thinking. Nor is there much more action when a person makes a speech or gives an interview thoughtfully setting forth his views on a public issue. Nor is there much action when antagonists sit down together and try to resolve their differences and reach an agreement. There is, however, a great deal of action when a public official makes a demagogic speech and stirs a crowd to applause and cheers. Action abounds when a small group of people organize a protest and march up and down in front of the Capitol or some other public building carrying signs and shouting their grievances. There is still more action if the police rush in swinging clubs, arrest the demonstrators, and throw them into paddy wagons. And action is supreme when there is a full-blown riot, some shooting and arson and looting, and best of all when there is a battle with guns being fired, fear registering on the faces of the combatants, and dead and wounded bodies lying around.

The need for action film creates an apparently irresistible thrust on television news toward depiction of demagoguery, dissension, and violence. Even though such film may fill only a minute or two of a half-hour newscast otherwise devoted to peaceful, constructive news, the shots of violence are the best film. They have the most impact on the viewer. They are remembered far longer than film of the president expressing his hopes for the brotherhood of mankind. For all of these reasons, the need for action film on television news has an incalculable and mostly odious effect on why we think as we do. The way we think about ourselves, our nation, and the world is irrevocably shaped by the demands of television to have action film.

Television also distorts the news because of its "show biz" aspects. Most people become nervous and suffer stage fright at the prospect of appearing on television. The kleig lights, the camera and sound equipment, the members of the crew, are a little frightening. Even poised people become unnatural. This is precisely why all cameras are banned from courtrooms. Witnesses become upset and juries are influenced. Congress does not allow television inside the Senate and House chambers except on rare occasions, such as a presidential address. Television is barred from most labor-management collective bargaining sessions, most legislative meetings, board rooms, and similar places where frank, honest actions are desired. In fact, TV may be barred from more places than it is permitted.

There is a reverse side to this that is much commented on. Television gives an unfair advantage to the person who is slender, photogenic, poised, and experienced before the camera. The person who is even a little overweight, less photogenic, nervous, and slightly less articulate will make a poorer impression on the home screen. Handsomeness and show-biz acumen were not particularly sought after in political candidates prior to television.

All of these problems are greatly compounded by the need for extreme brevity in television news. Only rarely is it possible to realistically present a news event in a few seconds or even a minute or two. And on truly complex economic, political, and social events a short presentation may be only confusing. A government official appears before the cameras with a statement. His remarks are edited to a sentence or two. His other remarks, reasoning and qualifying words, are omitted. Distortion occurred. To achieve, fairness and objectivity, an opposing viewpoint will be offered, which may be an extremely minor one. That person may even be the only one who holds it. Yet, it will be dignified with a few seconds on television. Confusion and the appearance of controversy are created.

There are some stories that are natural for television. They are done extremely well. Mostly they are events, predictable in advance, that are at a specific location and orderly, so cameras and sound equipment can be set up. Space shots and astronaut landings are superb on TV. Presidential speeches and news conferences are effective. A Congressional hearing comes across well. The televised hearing of the House Judiciary Committee considering articles of impeachment against President Nixon in 1974 was a landmark for television.

Certain types of complex, ongoing news stories are adaptable to television. The two-year Watergate story "worked" on TV. The events occurred mostly in Washington, at the White House, Capitol, and outside various courtrooms and in the homes of participants. The events were slow moving and highly predictable. Crews were able to be on hand where an event was likely to take place or where a person might be available for an interview. The day's events could be compressed into a few minutes of air time.

Television news has great difficulty reporting complex events. The national political conventions are distressingly difficult for television. There are hundreds of delegates to create confusion. It is most difficult for even the most astute and experienced reporter to separate the trivial from the important, the puff from the sub-stance. The windy, boring speeches drone on, while important decisions are being made elsewhere out of camera range.

Television has great difficulty with economic news—with two important exceptions. It can report rising food prices and high unemployment. Prices are reported through the device of a "monthly market basket report." A reporter and camera crew are sent to stores in major cities to buy a set list of items. When the bill is flashed on the cash register, it is reported as higher or lower than the previous month or year. Unemployment is reported by giving Labor Department statistics and illustrating it by sending a crew to film the lines at the state employment offices. A few persons in line receive an opportunity to describe their woes.

The problem is that showing higher food prices and unemployment lines in no way explains the causes of the events or illuminates possible solutions. Economics is called the "dismal science." This refers to the fact that it is little understood, subject thereby to much disagreement among experts, and very complex. It is probably not possible to present even a cursory explanation of the American economic system in less than an hour. To attempt to do so in a few seconds creates only confusion and apprehension.*

There are many other types of stories hard for television. Social problems such as race relations, poverty, inequality of education, are complex and thereby difficult for TV. Housing, mass transportation and the energy shortage are also complex and difficult. Pollution and protection of the environment are exasperatingly complex. Showing a belching smokestack and smog over a city may il-

---

* A businessman of my acquaintance tells of watching television news during 1974 and 1975 and being nightly alarmed about the nation's economy and fearful that his business might go under. Each day he came to his office at a small manufacturing firm and found greatly increased orders for his products. Despite the news, his business was increasing. This illustrates a problem of television. Brevity forces it to report the general. There is little time for the specific and the exception.

lustrate a problem, but hardly suggest a solution. The problems of the nation's system of criminal justice and our prison system are not easily portrayed on television. The root causes of the plight of our cities do not reduce themselves to film very well. Many experts believe that inequity of taxation is the basis of our urban and many other economic and social problems. This subject is next to impossible to film and explain briefly. (Indeed, try to compress the contents of this book into a few minutes on television.)

The result is an imponderable distortion of the news. Certain events that are adaptable to television are given extensive coverage and have great impact on public opinion, while other major problems are largely ignored. Examples are legion. Television is very good at covering a war—or seeming to. Camera crews can go along on skirmishes and film the noise and confusion, the wounded and dying. The event may only have been a minor engagement while a major battle occurred somewhere else, but the reporter can declare the filmed skirmish to be more important than it was or pontificate that it was typical of the fighting and dying of the war. Television can show the crying and weeping of loved ones, the burning buildings, the suffering of soldiers and civilians. The reasons for the war, its larger meanings, the strategy behind it, might be neglected, but TV is excellent at bringing the horror and brutality and futility of warfare into the homes of Americans. It did this for years during the war in Vietnam and eventually caused major changes in American attitudes toward the war. Support for it dwindled and opposition rose.

Television is superb at showing street demonstrations and protests. These usually occur at prearranged locations. Camera crews are at hand. If violence occurs (sometimes by prearrangement also) it is shown in living rooms, sometimes even as it is happening. Television carried a great volume of civil rights protests of the 1950s and 1960s and the antiwar demonstrations of the late 1960s and early 1970s. The scenes of violence had immense impact, and much disagreement and dissension was fomented. Gradually public attitudes gelled in favor of civil rights for Blacks and against the war in Vietnam.

One more example. The Watergate story, as has been pointed out, worked on TV and absorbed a tremendous amount of the evening news, as well as special prime-time programming, for over two years. It was an agonizing period for Americans, but during this time of extensive TV coverage, Mr. Nixon's popularity plummeted, he became absorbed in extricating himself from the Watergate morass, and public opinion gelled against him and in favor of his removal from office.

The point here is most definitely not whether television news performed a service or disservice by its extensive coverage of these events. The point is that TV did give such extensive coverage and did have such a tremendous impact on public opinion. The point is, also, that many, many other extremely important public issues do not and by the nature of television, cannot receive such coverage and therefore public opinion is given little or no chance to form on complex issues, such as poverty, energy shortages, urban affairs, pollution, housing, taxation, and many others.

Because of the very nature of television, great attention is focused on certain problems adaptable to the medium. Public opinion coalesces one way or another on the issue. Other problems, unadaptable to television, are ignored or portrayed in a very limited, confusing manner. As a result huge groups of people are never given the opportunity to express themselves and make their serious problems known on television and thus share in its great impact on public opinion. Any sort of orderly system of national priorities is made very difficult because public opinion has been distorted for or against a televised problem while another equally serious problem is unknown.

Worse, television news creates confusion and indecision. A competent understanding of complex events is rarely given. Problems are presented piecemeal. The interrelation of such matters as taxation, competing local governments, lack of planning, housing, educational inequities, and poverty in creating the urban problem is almost totally neglected. Being told the oil-producing nations have raised their prices again does not give any competent understanding of the energy shortage and what to do about it. Revelations of the latest evidence of a financial crisis in New York City and the machinations of public officials to resolve it do almost nothing to reveal the roots of the problem in poverty and the urban crisis, our creaking system of public welfare, tax inequities, banking practices, and strains on our federal system of government. The brevity of television news, its piecemeal reporting of complex events, creates more confusion than understanding, more indecision than public opinion.

In the last analysis, television does not so much report the news as make it. This is true of newspaper people, but it is a far greater problem for TV because of its brevity. The act of deciding who will be interviewed on the nightly news makes that person a newsmaker. The person being interviewed is not reporting an event so much as he is creating the event. Print journalists lessen this problem by quoting many people and by writing background and analyses of the news that put events into perspective. Television's brevity largely prohibits background and depth analysis.

Television reporters are aware of these problems. They are honest, responsible, highly professional people. They truly try to use their great power over public opinion wisely. Yet, the crucial fact remains that the medium of television itself, its shortage of time and the need for brevity, the limitations of the camera and microphone, the need for action film to make newscasts interesting, preclude any sort of comprehensive reporting of the day's news and illumination of problems.

No one is suggesting, even if it were possible, that television news be eliminated or curtailed. What can be done? One suggestion from TV newsmen (Walter Cronkite of CBS is a particular advocate) is that national news programs be expanded, at least to an hour each evening. This would relieve newscasters of some of the curse of brevity and perhaps encourage more comprehensive reporting of more news. It has not been done because of the great expense the three commercial networks would incur. Others have suggested more special news programs on specific topics in prime time. Less emphasis on the size of the audience watching a particular show and more emphasis on TV's responsibility to the American people to inform them might encourage better programming. Another idea is greater financial support for public broadcasting stations so they can provide more programs on controversial topics related to national and world problems. It is pointed out, also, that television news has been in existence little more than a quarter century. Its techniques for reporting the news are still developing.

Meanwhile, it is important for the person who receives all or even a substantial portion of his news from television to realize that he is receiving a grossly limited amount of news that is highly distorted as to content and meaning. Such a person is quite poorly informed, unless he or she reads a variety of newspapers, magazines, and books relating to public issues. We think as we do in large measure because of television news. We can alter our thinking by reading and listening to other media and thereby demand better, more comprehensive, more responsible television reporting.

CHAPTER EIGHT And Now, This Commercial Message. . . .

In large measure we think as we do because of advertising.* We are influenced directly and subtly, positively and negatively by it.

Few actions in American life are as omnipresent as advertising. It makes up a large proportion, sometimes more than half, of the contents of newspapers and magazines. So much advertising appears on radio and television that the Federal Communications Commission has had to limit the amount of advertising in ratio to the content of the programming. Rarely can we escape advertising. It confronts us constantly, on billboards and signs, on packaging, on the most commonly used products, from sound trucks and even in lobbies, elevators, and doctors' offices. Even when we look heavenward, we may see some skywriting.

Individual companies spend hundreds of millions of dollars a year on advertising. The sum total of it is many billions of dollars annually.

Modern advertising is largely an American invention and preoccupation. It appears in some form over most of the world, and the influence of American admen is obvious. Foreign ads are generally imitative, although sometimes they are an improvement on American techniques. Surely, however, no country devotes so much time, energy, talent, and human ingenuity to advertising.

Economists disagree on the role and importance of advertising in

---

* In this discussion it is necessary to name certain brands, products, companies, and advertisements. This in no way constitutes an endorsement. Nor does the omission of a product or company mean a lack of endorsement. Those named are solely illustrative. No opinion of any commercial product is intended.

American life. Conventional thinking is that there is so much advertising that it cancels itself out, leaving advertising with little or no effect on economic life. Manufacturers and purveyors of such diverse items as cars, soap, breakfast cereal, cosmetics, liquor, and appliances vigorously advertise their products, each saying theirs is the best. Use of the product will lead—as the case may be—to fame, fortune, beauty, sex appeal, happiness, respect of family and friends, and the good life. The claims are so exaggerated and so obviously false that people pay little attention to advertising. The sales generated by advertising are approximately matched by the losses caused by a competitor's advertising. The effect on the economy, according to conventional wisdom, is about zero, except for the money earned by those who prepare the advertising and the media who sell time and space.

Economist John Kenneth Galbraith disagrees. He, and others, argue that advertising is a powerful tool used by the modern business corporation to control demand for their products and services. Indeed, it must be assumed that business executives are not fools. They would not spend tens and hundreds of millions of dollars a year on advertising that accomplished nothing except to enrich admen and ad media. Any adman knows that there is only one measurement of an ad's success—that it sells its product. The ad may be talented, artistically pleasing, widely seen, and highly popular, but if it does not increase sales it is quickly withdrawn. Conversely, the ad may be poorly thought out and offensive to many people, but if the product it purveys continues to sell well, the ad is likely to be used for years. Indeed, some ad executives believe that the more annoying an ad the more effective it is. Many corporations have stated that their sales bear a direct relationship to the dollar amounts they spend on advertising. Other companies deliberately increase advertising if sales decline. There would seem to be at least some evidence to support Galbraith's thesis.

Admen disagree about the effectiveness of their own work. For every much-told tale of an advertising success—the soap that cleans like a "white tornado," the Volkswagen "Bug" that made a small car a vogue, Morris selling cat food, the placement of Arm & Hammer baking soda in the refrigerator to keep it "clean smelling"—there is an equal or great number of ads that failed. Admen on occasion get rather emotional about the beautiful, sensitive, artistic ads that everyone loved—only they didn't sell the product.

Advertising executives are quick to point out that an ad campaign cannot succeed if the product fails. A lavish expenditure on advertising may convince people to try a product once, but if most of those users don't like the product, no amount of advertising will sell it for long.

Ad people also point out that Americans, barraged by advertising appeals, are extremely ad-wise. Every gimmick of sight and sound has been used thousands of times. Every ploy to appeal to a person's pride, guilt, fears, and cupidity has been seen and heard. Admen have even tried simple honesty, humor, and deliberate understatement to sell a product—and worn that out because it worked. Any ad executive will state that it is extremely difficult to invent an ad that is new and appealing enough to stand out among the volume of advertising that numbs the eyes and ears. Even children learn, almost before they can talk, that what is seen on television advertising is unreal. A jar of Nestle's instant coffee does not really percolate coffee, a doll is not really that big, a toy is not quite as much fun as it seemed to be on the tube. Adults are even more skeptic.

Admitting all these faults and failings of advertising, the fact remains that it has a profound effect on why we think as we do. Mass advertising has greatly altered who Americans are and the way we think. Our values, even our morality, have greatly changed because of advertising.

The most serious charge against advertising is that it has captured the majority of news and entertainment media, a charge hotly denied. It is a subject we must examine.

Virtually all newspapers, magazines, radio and television stations are financially dependent upon advertising to stay in business. The purchase price of a newspaper or magazine is only a small portion of the revenue it earns. The bulk of the money comes from the sale of advertising space. In radio and television, virtually all revenue comes from advertising. Only the Public Broadcasting System and a handful of educational stations are exceptions. Even then, these public stations receive a great deal of revenue in the form of grants or gifts from large corporations.

The exceptions to the influence of advertising are worthy of mention. Among the print media, only books and scholarly journals carry no advertising. Among the entertainment media, the theater, movies, and the fine arts, such as music and the dance, do not depend on advertising. Rightly or wrongly, many writers and performers believe these media offer greater freedom of expression than other media dependent upon advertising for their financial existence.

How much do advertisers influence the content of newspapers and magazines, radio and television broadcasting? This is a sensitive question, hotly debated. Virtually to a person, newswomen and men in all media will ferociously resist any attempt by any advertiser to dictate the contents of the news or interfere in any way with their prerogatives in reporting it. Indeed, if asked by an advertiser, a reporter or editor may well do the opposite of what the advertiser wants just to demonstrate independence of him.

The history of journalism rings with many tales of journalists who have suffered great financial loss and even gone out of business rather than knuckle under to the demands of advertisers. A routine argument in newspaper offices is between the advertising manager and the editor over whether a story about a company activity qualifies as news to be reported or free advertising. If the advertising manager is to win, he had best be persuasive about the news value of the story.

These battles are even more severe on radio and television. Newspapers and magazines can butter up advertisers in the business and financial sections, declaring puff pieces to be news. Radio and particularly television news do not air much business and financial news. It would be extremely difficult for Walter Cronkite, for example, to broadcast an item about the opening of a new Sears Roebuck store.

Despite all the elaborate resistances to advertising control of news, the power of advertising still remains. No editor or reporter in print or broadcast media is going to deliberately criticize a major advertiser if he doesn't have to. The paper, magazine, or station's financial success and thus his or her job depend on advertising. Common sense suggests that it is silly to drive away advertisers needlessly. If the company or its officers make news, it will be printed no matter how embarrassing. But the editor or reporter may avoid going out of his or her way to dig up derogatory news.

Certain news tends to be printed or not printed because of the existence of advertising. Newspapers and broadcast stations frequently oppose telephone, electric, or other public utiliy rate increases. This shows the media to have the public interest at heart. And, utilities, being franchised to operate in a specific area, are a natural monopoly and cannot realistically withdraw their advertising. The media generally encourage and publicize any form of business expansion that creates more jobs, such as new factories, stores, and shopping centers. Government contracts are similarly publicized, along with highway construction, dams, government buildings, and other public works.

Those who see the news media as captives of advertisers point to the fact that journalists were slow and reluctant to expose industrial polluters, the lack of safety in many automobiles, excessive and deceptive interest charges by lending institutions, price gouging by retail stores, the decline of mass transit and rail passenger service, the unfair fees charged by some lawyers and doctors, needlessly bad housing provided by slum landlords, and many other abuses and problems. There may be many reasons for such failures —lack of knowledge, interest, time and space for such exposés.

Critics maintain, however, that the news media failed to pursue such stories vigorously because they collide with the vested interests of advertisers and thus the vested interests of the news media.

At least a portion of the influence critics see advertisers exerting over news media may be little more than a natural community of interest. Publishing newspapers and magazines, operating radio and television stations, are business enterprises, sometimes quite large ones. The TV networks are among the nation's larger corporations. Being businessmen, the owners of news media would understandably have many interests in common with other businessmen who are advertisers. At least some of the influence of advertisers may be only a meeting of the minds.

The influence of advertising on the news media is far less than its impact on entertainment, especially television entertainment. How much advertisers control the content of television shows is a matter of dispute, but there is little doubt the influence is considerable.

Most television shows are the property of individual producers, production companies, or the television networks. The individual stations and the networks control what shows are to be telecast and when. Every new TV show is a gamble. The producer or network invests large sums of money in filming or taping a first show, or pilot. The network accepts a certain number of new shows each season, gambling that they will be popular with viewers so as to attract advertisers. Various rating systems are employed to determine what percentage of the audience watches a particular show at a specified hour.

When a new show is prepared and being considered for television, either as a regular or special, it generally will be shown to advertisers in private screening. If an advertiser can be convinced to pay for all or part of the show, it will generally be aired. If advertisers do not wish to take a chance on a new show, the network may telecast it anyway, gambling that the show will catch on enough to attract a regular advertiser in the future or enough "spot" advertisers to justify keeping it on the air. An advertising spot is the single commercial lasting from ten seconds to a minute. This contrasts with the regular advertiser who sponsors a show and has his product identified with it. The price of spots as well as sponsorship varies with the time of day and the size of the audience watching the show. For example, a minute spot on the Super Bowl or World Series game costs a great deal more than a minute on "Meet the Press."

A show will go off the air for lack of viewer or advertiser interest. If a show has a large audience, advertisers will usually follow. But there have been cases in which popular shows went off the air because advertisers refused to be identified with them. A more common event is for advertisers, in effect, to veto shows, both specials and individual episodes in continuing series, because they are likely to be controversial or are in some way offensive to advertisers. Producers of even the most popular series must give some thought to the attitudes and desires of sponsors.

Far more common is for the television networks to rigidly control what shows are aired. It is almost reflex for networks to avoid any type of controversial or innovative programming that they believe might anger an advertiser or be hard to sell to advertisers or agents. There is considerable discussion about how much of this influence over TV programming comes from advertisers and how much from networks.

Television critics maintain that the influence of advertising accounts for the banality of the medium, the insipid game shows and situation comedies, and the violent crime and detective shows. According to this point of view, so little appears on television of genuine artistic or even entertainment merit because advertisers and networks want to avoid material that is different, let alone controversial. It is safer to sponsor a sports broadcast, giveaway shows, or shoot-'em-up whodunits than a drama of genuine dramatic appeal. Network officials and other defenders of television argue that the medium shows what people want to watch, that people are more interested in being entertained or distracted than in being inspired.

Putting the merits of this argument aside, a more serious question is to what extent television and the ubiquitous commercials influence Americans' attitudes and values. This is a matter of great dispute. It can perhaps only be said that no one really knows.

In its prize-winning "Of Black America" series in 1968, CBS aired a segment showing how black Americans were portrayed in the movies. With precious few exceptions, Blacks were shown in one of several ways: as evil villains; silly, empty-headed women; silly, scared men and children dominated by their wives and mothers; happy-go-lucky people with rhythm; dutiful slaves and servants who helped white folks out of their difficulties. Always, but always, Blacks were cast in servile roles. The point was made by CBS that decades of such treatment of Blacks in movies and on television led to the assumption that this is what Negroes are really like. Beginning in the late 1960s, Blacks began to be shown more realistically in movies and on television shows and commercials, that is, as genuine people with real problems and aspirations. They were portrayed in a variety of professions and careers, and as families. Attitudes toward black people and racial tensions began to improve at the same time. How much the greater respect for Blacks in entertainment and advertising contributed to this may not be known, but it surely had some impact.

Something similar happened with American Indians. For decades, the only good Indian in the movies or TV was a dead Indian. The native American was cast into stereotyped roles of villain, half savage, cruel, and subordinate to white people. When Indians began to be portrayed as people of dignity and courage, victims of oppression, greater compassion and understanding resulted. Another similarity is the treatment of women. They are now being portrayed as independent persons with careers, responsibilities, and problems of their own, rather than as weak creatures subservient to men. A greater respect for women began to occur. The dispute is the extent to which these altered portraits of minorities in entertainment and advertising caused the changed attitudes. Did the more realistic portrayals cause the change in attitudes, or did the portrayals result from the changed attitudes?

For more than fifty years, American moviegoers and television watchers have witnessed an almost incessant portrayal of violence in Westerns, whodunits, and war shows. The good guys may have always won and virtue may have always triumphed, but it is hard to deny that this constant portrayal and even glorification of violence cannot but help have had some effect. There are those who argue that the media may have discouraged violence by showing it to be cruel and self-defeating. Perhaps, but it is impossible to deny that there is a great deal of violent crime in the United States. Has our long portrayal of crime and violence had nothing to do with it?

Movies, television, and advertising have been doing something else for more than a half century, offering with few exceptions a totally unrealistic view of American life. A hit movie of the 1970s was "That's Entertainment," a delightful reprise of the old musicals made by the Metro-Goldwyn-Mayer movie studio in Hollywood. These productions were pure fantasyland. In the depths of the depression of the 1930s, when a quarter of the work force was unemployed and many people labored for pennies a day, there was Fred Astaire in top hat and tails dancing with Ginger Rogers—attired in sequins and furs—dining on caviar and champagne in Venice in the movie "Top Hat." Americans adored it in the 1930s and still do today. The dancing of Astaire and Rogers is superb. And when director Busby Berkley set a hundred or more dancers to doing "The Continental" in another Astaire-Rogers movie, "The Gay Divorcee," a viewer marvels forty years later.

Examples are almost infinite in number—the poor working girl who goes home to an apartment that would cost a fortune to rent and furnish; the out-of-work young man who drives a new car; the beautiful house in suburbia; the effortlessness of going to college; the stylish wardrobes; elegance, opulance, and luxury. Hollywood, television, and advertising have always dealt in such fantasies. Even the ordinary looks pretty good. Why? Everyone, or nearly everyone, knows it is fantasy. Yet, the make-believe touches a peculiarly American note. Since these shores were first colonized, a consistent theme of the American dream has been that the little person can aspire to and achieve fame, fortune, the good life. The movies and television play on this theme, portraying that which people can aspire to. It may be fantasy, but to an American it is also possible.

For a long time, foreign critics (and a few domestic ones) have accused Americans of being materialistic. We are said to have too strong a tendency to equate personal happiness with houses, cars, TV sets, telephones, appliances, furniture, and attire. The charge may be exaggerated, but certain it is that Americans have a lot of these things, work very hard to get them, and value them highly. The pursuit of money and what it will buy is important in American life.

Why is this so? It may be human nature. There is evidence that people all over the earth will spend any extra money they have on possessions. They would like more money so they can own more. In the United States this natural desire for possessions has been greatly increased through the art of advertising. In commercials, particularly on television, a house is not simply shelter, clothing a means of keeping warm and dry, a car a means of transportation, or food a source of nourishment. All are much more. They are symbols of status, power, and glory. They are sex objects and the embodiment of the good life. They are a means to be popular and gain both self-respect and the respect of others.

None of this is by accident. A great deal of thought, study, and effort go into any advertising campaign. A thorough study is made of why people use a particular product, what they think about it, what they want it to do, how they feel about it. Psychologists are called in to explain the fears and desires that underlie the motives of consumers. Colors and shapes of products and packaging are devised to be most pleasing. If a celebrity is to give a testimonial, studies are made of the public attitudes toward that person.

In the 1950s, writer Vance Packard reported the use of motivational psychology in advertising in his book *The Hidden Persuaders*. He reported, illustrating in depth, how psychology and market research were uniting to create a new type of advertising that actually created desires among viewers and readers. His thesis was denounced at the time and ever since by advertising executives. The most frequent argument is to cite all the advertising and products that fail. Advertising is said to reflect public attitudes, not create them.

Perhaps, but there is strong evidence of the power of advertising. An urge, indeed need, has been created among the American people through the power of advertising to make the human underarms not only hairless, but dry, odorless, and stainless. This is a fairly unique desire, little known in the rest of the world. It is hard to conceive that Americans would have come to this attitude without advertising. The hair on the American head should be some other color than natural, and never, never reveal a speck of dandruff. The skin must be made softer, smoother, unblemished, smell of a peculiar odor, and the failure for it to be so is to invite social ostracism and self-denigration. The reader can come up with his own list of ad-induced desires—superwhite teeth, a superwhite wash, a car that is either superpowerful or supereconomical on gas. Indeed, the word "super" entered the language via advertising.

None of this is particularly natural to the human condition. It is predominantly an American phenomenon—although it has spread to Western Europe—created by advertising. A number of other phenomena seem traceable to advertising, particularly that on national television, our most important national advertising medium. Our national youth craze and its companion, the denigration of age, have at least some of their roots in television. The causes of this are not hard to figure. Some lie in demography, the study of population. The United States experienced a "baby boom" in the late 1940s and 1950s. There was a tremendous increase in the birth rate, creating a bulge in the population that will last for more than seventy years. The bulge meant there was first a great increase in the demand for diaper services and other necessities for infants. Progressively, the populations of elementary, junior and senior high schools, and colleges increased. In the 1960s, teenagers and young men and women were the largest segment of the population. It is easy to predict that in a few years, middle age will be the largest and most important segment, and after that senior citizens will be in vogue.

Another factor is that merchandisers discovered in the 1950s and 1960s that teenagers had many billions of uncommitted dollars to spend. Because the teens lived at home, the money was not spent on staples such as food and shelter but in an entirely discretionary fashion, on clothes, cosmetics, phonograph records, snacks, and cars. Merchandisers and advertisers set out to garner as much of this teen money as possible. The adoration of youth and what some have called the "youth rebellion" followed.*

A companion to the youth craze was the fad for slenderness. Even a little fat was summarily declared ugly and harmful to health and social acceptance. The female curves that had inspired artists for centuries were now declared unsightly. The ideal female figure on American advertising became extremely thin, only bone and muscle—except that through some miracle of nature the thin

---

* The youth craze in advertising was particularly deadly for a number of celebrated magazines that had been identified with middle-aged or blue-collar pursuits. Among these were *Coronet, Colliers, American, Saturday Evening Post, Life,* and *True.* These and other periodicals either went out of business or declined financially. Some have been resurrected in a new format. There were many causes for the decline of magazines, but an important one was that advertisers wanted to appeal to young, dynamic readers. Such magazines as *Playboy, Seventeen, Teen,* and *Cosmopolitan* flourished, while those identified with older readers did not.

girl was to have a large bosom. Since it is almost impossible for the female to be both fatless and bosomy, a generation of American women was set to pursuing a nearly impossible dream. Dieting became a craze. An alarming rise in the incidence of *anorexia nervosa,* a disease in which people cannot or will not eat, was recorded. As a companion to dieting, advertising was employed to peddle an array of vitamins, food supplements, and nostrums to maintain health that excessive dieting would otherwise destroy.

Many other illustrations might be given and all would point to the power of advertising, the impact it has on our lives. The fact that an individual advertising campaign may fail does not alter the fact that the sum of all advertising is a pervasive influence on why we think as we do. Not only has advertising altered our buying habits and thereby our personal definitions of our own wants and needs, it has fostered a great increase in total consumer demand and thus altered our economic system.

Advertising has created a consumer demand for the frivolous and nonsensical, and sometimes even for the harmful. If the necessities of life are food, clothing, and shelter, then most of the national advertising on network television is for nonessentials. There is very little national housing advertising. What little there is advertises vacation or retirement homes. There is somewhat more advertising for clothing, mostly by the large retail chains, such as J. C. Penney and Sears Roebuck. Suits, jeans, shirts, blouses, and shoes are necessities.

There is a great deal of food advertising on TV, but most of it is for breakfast cereal, frozen dinners, carbonated beverages, and a bewildering array of snacks. How essential these products are to human subsistence is questionable. (Also a great deal of television advertising is for soaps, cosmetics, deodorants, vitamins, laxatives, pain remedies, and other patent medicines. The manufacturers and admen constantly cite their usefulness. How necessary they are is again questionable. Repeated medical studies deny the usefulness of many of these products.

Some rather serious problems have resulted from advertising. So much clever advertising was done on cigarette smoking that a national health hazard resulted. Tobacco advertising was banned from broadcasting, although not from print media. Some people concerned about the rise of alcoholism urge the banning of beer, wine, and liquor advertising. The joys of the automobile, particularly large, powerful, ornamental, gas-guzzling ones, were purveyed so long and so often that the United States developed an energy shortage. The government is trying to come up with some formula to induce Americans to use less gasoline. For years, appliances, air conditioning, and other devices for using electricity have been heavily advertised. Now there is a shortage of electric power.

The charge is made that advertising and merchandising have led to great waste of natural resources and pollution of the environment. Cars and trucks were promoted, and the nation's mass transit and rail transportation allowed to decline, in some places to the point of extinction. The use of oil was promoted for home heating, and studies of better uses of coal neglected. Garbage collection and disposal became a national problem with plastic, glass, and paper packaging—much of it covered with advertising—threatening to mar the planet forever. Life in suburbia, reached by car, was glorified. The inner cities were allowed to deteriorate and nearly $100 billion was spent on superhighways to speed the flight to the suburbs.

The impact of advertising on the economic system occurred in another but profound way. Advertising, particularly on network television, costs a great deal of money. A single commercial may cost tens of thousands of dollars for air time and as much or more to produce. The distinguished actor, Sir Laurence Olivier of Britain, was induced to plug Polaroid Land cameras when he was paid several hundred thousand dollars for a few days' work. A single corporation may spend hundreds of millions of dollars advertising its products.

There is little or no place in all of this for the little or even moderate-sized business. The result has been a massive consolidation of American business and industry. The small family farm has given way to the agribusiness. The "mom and pop" restaurant, hamburger stand, and store have been replaced by the restaurant chain, the supermarket chain, the department-store chain, the dime-store chain. There is no way the corner garage can compete with Midas or Rayco in terms of advertising automotive repairs. It is impossible for even the best-run quick-service restaurant to compete in terms of advertising with McDonald's, Burger King, Howard Johnson's, Arthur Treacher's Fish 'n Chips, and a dozen others.

We have arrived at the era of the franchise store. To market a new line of frozen foods, a beverage, or open a national magazine and newspaper in the face of nationally advertised competition, is extremely difficult. Imagine trying to start a fifth automobile company in the United States. The consolidation of American industry and business, the growth of conglomerates, have increased greatly in the age of advertising. One may argue over whether that is good or bad, but it is difficult to substantiate that bigness has not occurred.

The economic system has been altered by advertising in still another way. The American middle class, long the bedrock of the economic system, has come under a tight squeeze. The middle class is by far the most heavily taxed by the federal and state governments. At the same time the middle class is expected to buy the houses, cars, appliances, and nonessentials plugged incessantly by advertising. That the middle class does not have enough money for all of these products has become increasingly obvious in terms of inflation and recession in the 1970s. The entire economy has been geared to a high level of middle-class consumption—all fostered by advertisements importuning Americans to spend more, buy more. When the money is simply not available for such purchases—or when people become resistant to advertised frills—sales drop, production declines, workers are laid off, and economic recession begins.

One final point. In the 1970s, Americans and their governmental leaders became extremely concerned about the causes of inflation. The price of everything seemed inevitably to rise. In the mid-1970s, prices were rising at double-digit rates, that is, more than 10 percent a year. The United States experienced a serious recession in 1974–75, the worst since the 1930s. Inflation was considered a leading cause.

There were many causes for the inflation. A leading one was said to be the quadrupling or quintupling of oil prices by oil-exporting nations, mostly in the middle East. In an industrial society seemingly everything runs on oil and oil products. The cost of everything thereby rose.

Yet, many economists were seeing another cause—the rise of personal expectations. Everyone seemed to expect more money this year than last and to spend more, acquiring more and more possessions. Great investments were made in homes, encouraged by realtors and banks who assured buyers that the price of homes had risen consistently since 1945 and would continue to do so.

Everyone seemed to have an inflated idea of how much money they needed to live on and how much another person earned. Tales of entertainers, athletes, and even an occasional writer receiving hundreds of thousands of dollars, even millions, a year, helped foster the notion that money—lots of money—brought the "good life," happiness, and social esteem. How much advertising, merchandising, and news puffery encouraged these attitudes may be open to dispute, but some effects can hardly be denied.

Advertising and its cousin, public relations, have had a serious effect on the nation's political and social systems. We consider this aspect of why we think as we do in the next chapter.

CHAPTER NINE   The Making of Images

In the 1960s, I was assigned by *True* magazine to do an in-depth profile on former Governor Leroy Collins of Florida. He had recently made a great deal of news as a troubleshooter for Presidents Kennedy and Johnson. He had successfully negotiated settlement of an explosive racial situation in the South and had averted a nationwide strike. Governor Collins was expected to run for the Senate from Florida and was even being mentioned as a vice-presidential candidate.

Governor Collins was very generous with his time. I followed him through most of one whole day. We talked until late at night at his home in Washington. I arrived back at his home early the next morning to ride with him to the NBC studios where he was to appear on the "Today" show. At that early hour, the governor was obviously tired. No longer a young man, he seemed draped in fatigue. His face was as gray as the leaden sky. Yet, when he arrived at the studio and had alighted from his car, he shook off his weariness and bounded into the studio full of energy, smiling, shaking hands and greeting people with enthusiasm. During his television interview, he projected vigor and command.

This is an example of the ability of public people to turn on a public face. A successful politician, regardless of how he feels, must be able to project a certain image when greeting the public. The image is usually a compendium of dignity, vigor, enthusiasm, personal warmth toward people individually and collectively, command, and statesmanship. Every reporter who has ever traveled with a political candidate has seen this public-face phenomenon.

Actually, everyone does it. We all have company manners in front of strangers, neighbors, and acquaintances. We are more truly ourselves with close family and friends. This phenomenon is perhaps most highly developed among show business people. Entertainers are expected to perform regardless of how they feel or their emotional problems. It is "the show must go on" tradition.

In many cases the image of a public figure is quite close to his or her real personality. The person is natural and genuine, perhaps needing only to force himself, as Governor Collins did that morning, to overcome fatigue and project vigor not truly felt. Sometimes, however, the public image is quite a bit different from reality. In 1974, Americans were shocked to discover the truth behind the image of Representative Wilbur D. Mills of Arkansas. He was chairman of the House Ways and Means Committee and often called the most powerful man in Congress. During a long career he had projected statesmanship, dedication, and personal rectitude. The shock came when a series of escapades with a striptease dancer was revealed. Mr. Mills hospitalized himself, confessing that he was an alcoholic.

The fact that the most powerful person in Congress, the individual most responsible for writing our tax legislation, was a secret alcoholic only illustrates a much larger problem. In simplest terms, how much do we know about the people we elect in this democracy of ours? As we see and listen to the officeholders and candidates, are we encountering the real individual who will lead us, or a carefully nurtured image of him devised by advertising, public relations, and merchandising experts more accustomed to purveying soap and cereal? Do we think as we do about the individuals who run for and hold office—from the president on down—because we have come to know and respect them, or because we have been bamboozled wholly or in part by a cleverly designed image that conceals the real person? Do we vote for a person or a mirage in hopes it will turn out to be real?

Whatever the correct answer might be, the simple fact is that among politicians considerable effort goes into a candidate's image, especially if a major office is being sought. The candidate will meet with his advisers, who usually include people from the advertising and public relations fields. With considerable care, an image of the candidate will be prepared, one which, it is hoped, is true, but certainly one the candidate can portray with ease. There are many images. Some of the more common ones are the dignified statesman, the experienced leader, the reformer, the folksy man of the people, the vigorous new face in politics, the incorruptible person of integrity.

Whatever image is projected, it is designed at least in part to fit the candidate's situation and the perceived mood of the voters. An incumbent is inevitably a person of experience running on his or her record. The challenger is a new face or a reformer. If the public is concerned about corruption in government or rule by political bosses, it is likely that both candidates will project themselves as honest men free of boss rule.

The image is carefully nurtured. The aim is to avoid having the candidate caught off guard, acting or saying something that confounds the image. To this end, the candidate is carefully coached and advised. His speeches and even his "extemporaneous" remarks are carefully prepared. He is coached on the issues, which to pursue, which to ignore, and what ideas to project on all of them. His appearances are carefully controlled. A man of the people may be seen often shaking hands on the street. A statesman may appear at more formal gatherings making formal speeches on the issues. If the candidate is photogenic and articulate, he may appear often on television, while another candidate, feeling awkward before cameras, may avoid it as much as possible and even go to some lengths to appear bumbling and inept so as to project himself as a person inexperienced in these matters. This image is a ploy for sympathy, and it has worked many times.

The candidate's advertising, the billboards, posters, and signs will all be tied in with the image. An effort will be made to control all photographs of the candidate, so the image is never confounded. Even "candid" photos are sometimes posed. One of the most famous political photos ever taken was of Adlai Stevenson, the Democratic presidential nominee in 1952. He was shown preoccupied with reading, his legs elevated to reveal holes in the soles of his shoes. The instant image was of a common man of the people, a natural person, an honest man more interested in comfort than in appearances. The shot was later revealed to have been posed.

Much more is posed. In his book, *The Selling of the President, 1968* Joe McGinniss provided a behind-the-scenes report on the advertising and public relations for President Nixon's 1968 campaign. Reviewers used such words as "gruesome" and "frightening" to describe the machinations of advertising and public relations image makers.

At least nominal deference was paid to Mr. Nixon as the presidential nominee, yet his coterie of advisers went to elaborate lengths to control his every appearance, particularly on television. The staging was contrived. The citizens who questioned him during television appearances were handpicked. The "selling" of Mr. Nixon to the American people was done almost precisely as the same people would sell a cake of soap or a box of breakfast cereal. Perhaps the most revealing quote in McGinniss's book was the following from one of Mr. Nixon's top advertising managers:

> Let's face it, a lot of people think Nixon is dull. Think he's a bore, a pain in the ass. They look at him as the kind of kid who always carried a bookbag. Who was forty-two years old the day he was born. They figure other kids got footballs for Christmas, Nixon got a briefcase and he loved it. He'd always have his homework done and he'd never let you copy.

> Now you put him on television, you've got a problem right away. He's a funny looking guy. He looks like somebody hung him in

a closet overnight and he jumps out in the morning with his suit all bunched up and starts running around saying, "I want to be President." I mean this is how he strikes some people. That's why these shows are important. To make them forget all that.

Is this adman putting down the man who became president—or is he putting down himself, his values, his contempt for the American people?

American political campaigns have always been colorful, filled with a certain amount of deception and dishonesty. During our first century or more as a nation, votes were bought and sold. Campaign contributions were extorted from government employees. Open violence was a feature of election day. Yet, modern image building was little known. In the election of 1876, the Republican nominee was Ohio Governor Rutherford B. Hayes. His Democratic opponent was Samuel J. Tilden, governor of New York. Both men were nominated at their respective national conventions. Neither man campaigned, for it was considered unseemly for the man to seek the office. It had to be bestowed on him. Hayes and Tilden wrote letters, gave interviews, and advised their party national committees, who did all the campaigning. The closest either came to campaigning was to appear at the Centennial Exposition in Philadelphia to open their respective state exhibitions.

The contrast with the 1976 election can hardly be more sharp. Gerald Ford and Jimmy Carter spent a year campaigning in state primaries. Each spent tens of millions of dollars, campaigning incessantly, most of it on advertising and air time for speeches. Each was surrounded by a cadre of advisers, managers, advance men, and media specialists.

The entry of media image makers into politics may have its advantages, but some serious repercussions are evident. It might be suggested that the tremendous exposure a modern candidate receives on television would help the American people know that individual better and thus make a wiser choice in the election. But it must be said that the people did not truly know either of the last two men elected president (President Ford having been appointed Vice-president and then elevated to President).

Both Lyndon Johnson and Richard Nixon had a penchant for secrecy and surprise. Both presidents seemed to relish secret schemes, which they would delight in revealing to the surprise of nearly everyone. There were many examples: Mr. Johnson's escalation of the war in Vietnam and his sending troops into the Dominican Republic; Mr. Nixon's invasion of Cambodia and his startling reversals of economic policies. The point is not whether secrecy and surprise were wise or necessary, but rather that the tendencies of both men toward these qualities were not revealed when they campaigned. Rather, the image of both men was of consistency of principle.

The entry of advertising and public relations techniques into politics had a more serious effect—the opportunity for corruption, graft, and the abuse of power. Advertising, particularly on television, costs a great deal of money. An estimated $400 million was spent in the 1972 local, state, and federal elections, including about $60 million for Mr. Nixon's reelection bid. Many observers believe that campaign financing, the raising of such huge sums, was a root cause of the Watergate scandal. Much of Mr. Nixon's campaign chest came from illegal sources or was incorrectly reported or was hidden from public knowledge. At least some of the money was given in hopes of gaining ambassadorships and other federal positions, of currying favor with government agencies, of obtaining favorable policies and actions from the White House.

One of the articles of impeachment voted against Mr. Nixon was that attempts were made to illegally influence agencies such as the Internal Revenue Service, Federal Bureau of Investigation, and the Central Intelligence Agency. Campaign money was clearly used to pay burglars who broke into the Democratic National Committee headquarters in the Watergate complex. Among the fallout from the scandal were revelations that many candidates of both parties had abused campaign finance laws. Congress has enacted reforms designed to limit spending in presidential campaigns and to control how the money is spent.

The image making continues after the president takes office. Indeed, it intensifies. The appearances of the president, both on television and in public, are carefully staged to present a desired image of him and to enhance his policies and actions. In no small way do we think as we do about the president, his actions, our government and nation because of the careful stagecraft that surrounds our every glimpse of the president and because of the ceremonial trappings that have come to surround the chief executive. We need to take a look at some of these regal-like trappings and how they grew.

The modern president is benefited or afflicted, depending on the point of view, by almost 200 years of traditions and customs that have grown up around the office. George Washington initiated the office, bringing the dignity and command that were natural to him as a person. Most of his successors have been hard pressed to measure up to him. Washington's very presence, his impeccable integrity, won instant respect. Yet, he was a simple man. During a trip as president, he was accompanied only by a valet. When he stopped for the night, Washington would alight from his carriage and personally inspect the inn to see if the room was clean and the accommodations suitable. When a modern president travels, he is accompanied by scores of assistants, Secret Service agents, and journalists. Wherever he stays must be closely checked and guarded. Elaborate communications equipment must be installed. For a president to check into a public hotel or motel for the night is unthinkable.

The modern president lives and works in the White House, a mansion of tremendous size. He has a luxurious retreat at Camp David in Maryland. His personal home or vacation site may undergo many improvements. Mr. Nixon had homes at San Clemente, California, and Key Biscayne, Florida. Large sums of tax money were spent on installing communications and protective equipment, as well as office space. The president travels in a fleet of jet planes,* helicopters, and automobiles. There is a presidential yacht. A staff of thousands assists him and his family. When he appears in public, the presidential flag and seal are displayed and "Hail to the Chief" is rendered by a military band.** Mr. Nixon was scoffed at when he sought to attire the White House police in fancy ceremonial uniforms. The clothing reminded people either of a royal court or comic operettas. The laughter led Mr. Nixon to discard his plan.

Many people believe these traditions and trappings benefit the chief of state of a powerful nation. Other people see them as evidence of "the imperial presidency," a term used by Arthur M. Schlesinger, Jr., in a book by that title. Another criticism is that the trappings make the president too removed from the people, accessible only to a coterie of sycophants who surround him.

There is evidence that the imperial trappings of the presidency are of rather recent origins. Mrs. Anna Roosevelt Halsted, daughter of President Franklin D. Roosevelt, spent a great deal of time in the White House during her father's administrations from 1933 to 1945. In a conversation, she described life as very simple and informal. She said her father gave orders to avoid any unnecessary expense or ostentation. The nation was mired in the Great Depression, then enmeshed in World War II. He felt that even the ap-

---

* In the November 24, 1975, issue of *Time* magazine, reporter Hugh Sidey offered this account of life aboard Air Force One, the presidential plane: "Crew members lather that beautiful plane with Glass Wax before a trip, polish it to a mirror finish with compressed-air buffers, and add tire black to the ten wheels. They fill the hold with the tenderest chicken and juiciest steak, packing it all away in dry ice with flawless precision so that each day's meals come up on top in proper order. On board, far above the world's anguish, life is eased by soft stereo and fingertip service from six stewards. Who could resist?"

** In an effort to reduce the trappings of the office, President Ford replaced many renditions of "Hail to the Chief" with the University of Michigan fight song. Mr. Ford was an all-American football player at the university.

pearance of luxury was inappropriate. Roosevelt liked simple food and informality. Even at formal state dinners, she said, the food was simple—and some criticism was made of that.

Harry Truman, who succeeded FDR, was if anything an even more modest individual. A spate of books and a play about Truman are filled with tales of his plainness. One scene in the play shows Mr. Truman buying a three-cent stamp, licking it and affixing it on a personal letter. It is said of Mr. Truman that he carried his luggage into the White House and carried it out. His first act upon returning to his home in Independence, Missouri, in 1953 was to carry the suitcases up to the attic.

Dwight Eisenhower, who followed Mr. Truman, was also a man of simple tastes, but the trappings began to grow with him. He was a five-star general, accustomed to command and to the assistance of a large staff. The number of White House personnel grew, along with the practice of having powerful assistants who insulated the President from routine matters. Air Force One, the presidential plane, was outfitted. Camp David was built as a presidential retreat and named after David Eisenhower, the President's grandson. Frequently in ill health, Mr. Eisenhower vacationed often and was visible on golf courses.

But it was John F. Kennedy, both in his administration and in his assassination, who gave a big thrust toward imperial trappings. Both Mr. Kennedy and his attractive wife, Jacqueline, brought elegance to the White House. They held many state dinners, teas, and concerts. The White House tended to become a social center for the nation. Mrs. Kennedy's clothes were the subject of much attention and widely copied. When President Kennedy was assassinated in 1963, the nation's mourning was suffused with pride at the courage and dignity of Mrs. Kennedy and her children as seen at the televised funeral rites. Europeans dubbed Mrs. Kennedy the "queen of America."

Presidents Johnson, Nixon, and Ford, and their wives, have all been less wealthy and less patrician than the Kennedys. These successors have therefore been somewhat hard-pressed to maintain the aura of elegance and culture of the Kennedy "Camelot." It has been reported that both Mr. Johnson and Mr. Nixon felt a sense of competition with the Kennedy ghost in this regard. Certain it is that before Mr. Kennedy, presidents and their wives were not particularly expected to be clothes models. Eleanor Roosevelt, Bess Truman, and Mamie Eisenhower were widely admired as women. They were not expected to set fashion trends.

Presidential image making began to increase in other, more serious ways. Roosevelt, who was a polio victim and unable to walk without crutches, asked reporters not to photograph him on crutches or in a wheelchair. He seldom was, while many photos were taken of his celebrated smile and vigorous wave of the hand. Truman cast an image with his famous morning walk, or "constitutional," his feisty "give 'em hell" style of campaigning. Eisenhower offered his wide, cherubic grin, his V-for-victory sign and his "I like Ike" buttons.

Such devices seem naive today compared to more recent efforts at imagery. One thinks of Lyndon Johnson's special podium so the words of his speech passed (unseen by the audience) in front of him so he did not have to look down or appear to be reading. Or, Richard Nixon, under great pressure to reveal the contents of his White House tapes concerning the Watergate scandal, doing so, or pretending to, on national television. While he spoke, saying he was revealing all to finally settle the matter, the camera panned over a large stack of blue-bound books said to be transcripts of the mysterious tapes. Examination showed the transcripts to be heavily edited, with much material expurgated.*

---

*Some of the more salty language was replaced with the words, "expletive deleted." This term entered the language as a joke to replace the use of cuss words.

Gerald Ford also experimented with television imagery. Soon after taking office, he employed some experts to improve his television techniques. Thus, in one speech he stood up and walked around his office, lounged on the edge of his desk, and turned dramatically to look into a different camera in the manner of a television commentator or actor in an advertising commercial. It was an exercise in studied informality. In another speech he sought to dramatize the fact that Congress had not enacted his energy policies by ripping, one by one, the pages off a calendar to illustrate the time over which Congress had failed to act. Mr. Ford served in Congress for twenty-five years, much of it as House minority leader. He knew that the Congressional inaction reflected the divisions among the American people on how to solve the energy problem. Yet, he chose an image that sought to denigrate Congress, a coequal branch of government, while proposing his own decisiveness. Mr. Ford's imagery may or may not have improved his political position—but it certainly encouraged distrust of the American form of government.

The White House press conference has long been a vehicle for presidents to state their views while being questioned by journalists. These used to be highly informal affairs held in the president's office. Beginning with Kennedy, the press conference began to be televised and formalized. The conference began to be a vehicle for the president to address the nation and, in the view of many journalists, thereby deteriorated. The public relations aspects of the televised press conference were well explained by John Osborne, a veteran correspondent for *The New Republic:*

Numerous reporters and commentators forgot that the controlling function of the White House press secretaries and other official spokesmen is not to tell the truth. It is to put the best possible appearance upon what their principals do and say and, if necessary in the course of that endeavor, to conceal the truth. What my brethren in the White House pressroom were really celebrating, during the halcyon interlude that ended with the pardon of Richard Nixon, was the departure of Mr. Nixon and the quaint illusion that concealment and deception departed with him.

Imagery and deception are pervasive throughout much of American life. The Arab oil boycott in 1973 resulted both in a severe gasoline shortage in the United States and huge profits for the American oil companies. These corporations, which had been advertising to sell their products, immediately switched to "institutional" type ads and public relations statements contending that the high profits were needed to invest in searches for new oil wells. Many charities promote their life-saving activities, particularly as they pertain to children, while neglecting to report the often high percentage of gifts spent for promotion, collection, and administration. Many labor unions frequently cite the plight of the workingman, yet fail to tell the full truth about their own make-work activities, involvement with gangsters, and secret collusion with management.

All such activities, motivated by self-interest, conceal the truth from the American people. Solutions to collective national problems become more difficult because of the clamoring of individual or corporate interests. An orderly system of national priorities becomes distorted by the talent of public relations experts and the money spent for their endeavors. Serious problems tend to be reduced to self-serving symbols, slogans, and rhetoric.

Worse, the deception has led to an aura of distrust among the American people. Unable to tell truth from distortion, many people have succumbed either to apathy or to a cynicism in which no one is wholly believed. Not all, certainly, but many people tend to distrust presidential statements or at least look for an underlying motive. These negative attitudes have long reduced the effectiveness of advertising and public relations activities by business firms. The extension of such feelings to government may be viewed with sadness. No particular clairvoyance is required to suggest that the American people have a great longing for leaders who speak to them frankly, honestly, clearly, and guilelessly about the nation and its problems. Personal integrity inspires confidence. Public relations imagery leads to doubt.

CHAPTER TEN   Why We Think As We Do

There are many types of maps of the United States. A political map shows the states and cities; a topographical map the mountains, plains, and rivers; an economic map the principal agricultural and industrial areas. There are climatic and population maps.

It might also be possible to draw what might be called an "influence map." It might show a large area on the West Coast called Los Angeles, a big area on the East Coast called New York, with the rest of the country being called Washington, D.C. Such a map would reflect the fact that these three areas develop most of our national news, most of our television, movie, and theater entertainment, most of our national advertising and related activities. A great many of our largest corporations and financial institutions are housed in one or more of these places. Our principal stock exchanges are in New York City. It is a center for book and magazine publishing.

Many people are critical of this concentration of news reporting, entertainment, and advertising activities. A famous critic is former Vice-President Spiro T. Agnew who said reporters and broadcasters were guilty of "elitist" thinking because they see each other so often and question the same news sources.

The concentrations of influences on public opinion would seem to be inevitable. A great deal of news is going to be made in the national capital, be it Washington or Keokuk, Iowa. The communications center for a television network, the sound stages for movie making, have to be centralized somewhere. It might as well be New York and Los Angeles.

There are problems associated with this concentration of influence. Linguists decry the effects of the neutral voices of broadcasters on the colorful dialects and accents of America. Many people fear that regional speech and pronunciation are giving way to the standardized speech heard on radio and television. Another worry is that the English language is being drastically altered by the jargon frequently written and uttered by government officials and academicians. It is a language compiled of words borrowed from sports, computer programming, and space programs—liberally splashed with words that sound important. The aim of this language is to confuse and conceal meaning (or the lack of meaning) from the person not initiated into this special tongue.

There is a far more serious problem, one that is double-edged. Customs, attitudes, and life-styles in New York, Washington, and Los Angeles are not necessarily those of the rest of the country. In fact, they are frequently quite different. A midtown Manhattan cocktail party, a tennis-swimming bash in Beverly Hills, a conference in Washington, are not exactly the common experiences of most Americans. Most of us lead simpler lives. Our day-to-day concerns are not how to get on the "Johnny Carson Show," how to get a sports or entertainment celebrity to plug a product, or the attiudes of senators toward a piece of legislation.

One edge of the problem is that the mores of the influence centers may be thrust upon the entire country. A popular daytime game show is "Match Game." A contestant from a small town in Arkansas appeared one day. The emcee, Gene Rayburn, asked her if she watched the show back home. She replied, "Oh, yes, but we consider it risqué." The sort of double entendre, sex-obsessed questions on that and a dozen other game and talk shows on television may be great for laughs in Los Angeles or New York, but they are often embarrassing in other parts of the country. There is a risk that the moral or at least verbal standards of Hollywood and Manhattan may become nationalized.

The other edge is that the news, entertainment, advertising, and other molders of public opinion may become so out of touch with the mass of the population that they cease to have much influence. Some evidence exists that something like this may be happening. There is a fairly significant underground press in the United States. News sheets, pamphlets, and books circulate in large numbers, frequently among people of extreme political views, either to the right or left, conservative or radical. A popular theme of this literature is that various conspiracies exist to subvert the nation. Radicals on the left believe the conspiracy is headed by wealthy individuals and corporations on the right. Radicals on the right believe Communists on the far left are the conspirators. The two sides frequently unite in suggesting that government officials, news media, and something vague known as "The Establishment" are covering up and supporting the overthrow of this country and the American way of life.

Other evidence is that a significant percentage of the population seems apathetic about government. Only 38 percent of the eligible voters went to the polls in the 1974 Congressional elections. The Bureau of Census reported in 1975 a sharp increase in the number of people leaving urban and suburban life to return to rural living. Census takers called it the largest decline in urban population since the first census in 1790. There are surely many motives, but one apparently is a desire to return to a simpler life where the person is more dependent upon the land and his or her own resources. Use of gadgets, appliances, and store-bought items is avoided as much as possible. Finally, there is the statistic that about 10 percent of the American people live abroad, many of them by choice.

Those who mold public opinion, especially newsmen and women, are conscious of this double-edged problem. They are trying hard to consider the effects of their actions upon people and to stay in touch with them to make their activities relevant.

Why do we think as we do? To summarize, the reasons are an amalgam of what each of us is as a person, our genetic instruction received from our parents and our forebears, our childhood experiences, the perceptions each of us receives from our life's experiences. All these factors make each of us unique. We think as we do because of this land we inhabit and the history of the people who discovered, populated, and built it and our form of government. Our history as a nation helps form us. It lives in each one of us.

We think as we do because of what we know and don't know—our information. That which happens in secret and is unknown to us has a profound effect even if it is unknown. Our information is received from the educational system and from our imperfect system of news distribution. We think as we do because of the myriad impressions and images thrust upon us by mass communications, advertising, public relations techniques, some of which have been expropriated into our political and economic systems.

Summarized another way, we think as we do in part because of what we are as a person and what we have learned and continue to learn. Some of that learning enhances and ennobles us. Other parts of it are self-serving to those who would manipulate our thinking and our opinions. It is the difficult task of all of us to tell the ennobling from the self-serving.

This is really the meaning of self-government in a democracy. How can we differentiate between the real and the false, fact and propaganda, the beneficial and the wasteful?

None of us is going to be one hundred percent successful in these tasks. All of us are going to be fooled some of the time. Yet, we can perhaps lower the incidence by being aware of propaganda techniques and the ways informational and image media deceive us. This book has tried to provide information in this regard.

We can place a measure of trust in our institutions of government. Our political system may be imperfect, but the simple fact is that it has served us well. France had its Napoleon, Germany its Hitler, Italy its Mussolini, Spain its Franco, the Soviet Union its

Stalin and his successors. Many other nations have succumbed to despotism.

Among the nations that have not is the United States in its 200 year existence. The founders feared it. The men who wrote the Constitution wrangled long over the powers of the president. In the end, they designed it for George Washington, the man who was chairman of the Constitutional Convention and whom they knew would be the first president. Benjamin Franklin, wise as always, said it best: "The first man at the helm will be a good one. No one knows what sort may come afterwards."

That "sort" has not come so far, which is no accident, for the founders built into the engine of government a system to prevent tyranny. James Madison, secretary to the Convention and later our third president, explained it in these words: "Ambition must be made to counteract ambition." The powers of government are spread over many offices, and thereby many people. Human nature and the ambitions of one person colliding with the ambitions of another have so far prevented despotism. Our system may make for a government that is slow to move, because the ambitious persons may have trouble agreeing. Injustice may continue for a seemingly unwarranted interval. Yet, our system prevents a tyranny that, however fast acting, could destroy us and our liberty.

Our system of government provides another protection against propagandists—the First Amendment of the Bill of Rights. It was quoted earlier in the book—our guarantees of freedom of religion, of speech, of the press, and the right to petition. America has remained free—amazingly so in the twentieth century—because of the guarantees of freedom of expression. The warning has been repeated twice in these pages. A third time will do no harm. The first act of those who would take away freedom is to commandeer the broadcast facilities and censor the press.

Free speech and free press, the ability of many voices to be heard and recorded, the free exchange of ideas and information, are our strongest guarantee of liberty, the biggest enemy of propaganda. Our biggest danger is censorship, either censorship by governmental constraint or censorship because only certain people can afford to buy advertising. Again, the free exchange of ideas is our protection. It is a sign of maturity, as a person and as a nation, that we permit people to say that which we disagree with.

To many people all of this is terribly naive. It is possible to cite many instances in which these freedoms have been bent and even squandered. Yet, battered and scarred, these freedoms have somehow stayed intact. They are the most important parts of our existence as Americans.

Yet, when a person considers all the nationalities that have in one way or another succumbed to propaganda, the ultimate protection against it is human nature, common sense, simple verities, truth—it has many names. A person knows, or soon discovers, when he or she is being lied to. Every person comes natively possessed with the ability to tell right from wrong, truth from deception. Those people who have remained free have been able to abide by what is natural to them as people.

In the summer of 1975, the nation of Portugal was racked by riots between Communists and anti-Communists for control of the nation. In the town of Braga, Roman Catholic Archbishop Francisco Maria da Silva addressed a crowd. Among his remarks were these:

> . . . We want respect for public morality and moral values. We want respect for fundamental human rights. Christian people must assume their responsibilities, certain that the best values guide their lives. . . .

Many other religions could be substituted for the word "Christian" and the message would be the same. Indeed, the reference to religion could be omitted, leaving it that *people* must assume their responsibilities.

The archbishop's cry for fundamental human rights is almost precisely that which motivated the people who founded the United States. Our words: "All men are created equal . . . endowed by their Creator with certain inalienable rights. . . ." The desire for fundamental human rights that inspired this nation apparently still inspires men of freedom today. This desire is a protection against propaganda.

NOTES

Pages 11–14.   The quoted words and phrases are from *The Idea Invaders*, by George N. Gordon, Irving Falk and William Hodapp, pp. 50–1.

Pages 29–30.   *The Nation* quote is from "War-making Machinery," August 17, 1970.

Page 51.   The quotations are from the August 4, 1975, issue of *Time*, p. 54.

Page 52.   The *Time* quote is from the same issue, p. 10.

Page 109.   The quotation is from *The Selling of the President, 1968*, by Joe McGinniss. This quote is from the Pocket Book edition, pp. 103–4.

Pages 116–117.   Mr. Osborne was quoted in "The Second Most Agonizing Job in the World," by Herbert G. Klein, in *TV Guide*, August 2, 1975, p. 3.

Page 124.   Archbishop da Silva was quoted in *Time*, August 25, 1975, p. 29.

BIBLIOGRAPHY

Andersen, Kenneth E., *Persuasion: Theory and Practice*. Boston: Allyn and Bacon, Inc., 1971.

Aronson, James, *Deadline for the Media*. Indianapolis: Bobbs-Merrill Co., Inc., 1972.

Bagdikian, Ben H., *The Information Machines*. New York: Harper & Row, Publishers, 1971.

Berelson, Bernard and Janowitz, Morris, *Public Opinion and Communication*. New York: The Free Press, 1953.

Boelcke, Willie, ed., *The Secret Conferences of Dr. Goebbels, The Nazi Propaganda War, 1939–43*. New York: E. P. Dutton & Co., Inc., 1970.

Chandler, Robert, *Public Opinion*. New York: R. R. Bowker Co., 1972.

Christenson, Reo M. and McWilliams, Robert O., *Voices of the People*. New York: McGraw-Hill Book Co., 1962.

Cirino, Robert, *Don't Blame the People*. New York: Random House, Inc., 1971.

Della Femina, Jerry, *From Those Wonderful Folks Who Gave You Pearl Harbor*. New York: Simon & Schuster, Inc., 1970.

Gordon, George N., Falk, Irving, and Hodapp, William, *The Idea Invaders*. New York: Hastings House, Publishers, Inc., 1963.

Key, V. O., Jr., *Public Opinion and American Democracy*. New York: Alfred A. Knopf, Inc., 1961.

Ladd, Bruce, *Crisis in Credibility*. New York: New American Library, Inc., 1968.

Lane, Robert E. and Sears, David O., *Public Opinion*. Englewood Cliffs, N.J.: Prentice-Hall, Inc., 1964.

Lang, Kurt and Engel, Gladys, *Politics and Television*. Chicago: Quadrangle Books, 1968.

McGinniss, Joe, *The Selling of the President, 1968*. New York: Trident Press, 1969.

Packard, Vance, *The Hidden Persuaders*. New York: David McKay Co., Inc., 1957.

————, *The Naked Society*. New York: David McKay Co., Inc., 1964.

Rivers, William L. and Schramm, Wilbur, *Responsibility in Mass Communication*. New York: Harper & Row, Publishers, 1969.

Schettler, Clarence, *Public Opinion in American Society*. New York: Harper & Brothers, 1960.

Stein, Robert, *Media Power*. Boston: Houghton Mifflin Co., 1972.

Wise, David, *The Politics of Lying*. New York: Random House, Inc., 1973.

Schlesinger, Arthur M., *The Imperial Presidency*. Boston: Houghton Mifflin Co., 1973.

INDEX

ABOUT THE AUTHOR

Robert A. Liston was born in Youngstown, Ohio. He received his B.A. from Hiram College, Hiram, Ohio, where he majored in history and political science. A reporter for many years and the author of more than twenty books, Mr. Liston is currently living in Connecticut. His other books published by Franklin Watts, Inc., are *The Limits of Defiance: Rights, Strikes, and Government, The Edge of Madness: Prisons and Prison Reform in America, The Right to Know: Censorship in America*, and *Patients or Prisoners? The Mentally Ill in America*.